Sonnets of the Commedia dell'Arte

A cycle of sonnets by Dominic Peloso

Adapting fourteen classic scenarios codified in 1611
by Renaissance playwright Flaminio Scala

**Dark
Mountain
Books**

ISBN: 978-1-931468-41-1
First Printing

Table of Contents

Introduction

WHAT IS A SONNET?

Sonnets are a traditional form of poetry dating back to the Middle Ages. A formal sonnet has fourteen lines, with ten (sometimes eleven) syllables per line, and uses one of a number of set rhyme schemes. The first sonnets were written in Italian in the 1300s. A famous early poet was Francesco Petrarca, who popularized a particular rhyme scheme now known as the Petrarchan Sonnet. Later poets used different rhyme schemes for various reasons – most famously Shakespeare, who designed the "Shakespearean Sonnet" to rhyme better with English words than the Petrarchan, which had been originally designed with Italian words in mind.

During the Middle Ages, sonnets were the most popular form of poetry, so if you've read any poems written in the 1400s, 1500s, or 1600s, they were probably sonnets.

WHAT IS A CROWN OF SONNETS?

Poets were always trying to outdo one another or add extra twists to make their work more challenging. So, someone sometime came up with the idea of a 'crown of sonnets,' which is a set of sonnets all on the same theme where the last line of the first sonnet is the same as the first line of the second sonnet, and so on in a big circle. That adds a little logistical complexity because you have to fit all the rhymes together in a way that makes sense, and it adds some creative complexity because you have to write multiple poems about the same general topic without getting boring and repetitive.

In 1460, a group of poets in Siena, Italy decided to take it one step further and write a crown consisting of fourteen sonnets, with the extra challenge that if you combine the first lines of each of the fourteen individual sonnets, it forms a secret fifteenth sonnet called a Mastersonnet. That's known as a Heroic Crown of Sonnets (aka Sonnet Redoublé).

What is a Heroic Crown of Crowns?

At some point, people started to theorize about an even greater challenge called a "crown of crowns." A crown of crowns consists of fourteen crowns of fourteen sonnets each, and then the mastersonnets from those fourteen crowns form a fifteenth crown on their own, and generate a fifteenth, master Mastersonnet, which is called the Grandmastersonnet. Thus, a crown of crowns consists of 196 unique, interlinked sonnets which generate fourteen Mastersonnets which generate a single Grandmastersonnet for a total of 211 sonnets.

This was generally considered to be a ridiculous and impossible task and has only been accomplished a few times in the entire history of world literature.

Why have so few Heroic Crown of Crowns been written?

The main reason is that very few people write formal poetry anymore. Since the early 1900s, almost all poets write free-verse, which doesn't have the constraints of rhyme and meter, so there's probably a lot of modern poets that have the ability to write a heroic crown of crowns, they just don't have any desire to do so.

There are three particular challenges in writing a heroic crown of crowns. The first challenge is that, logistically, it is hard to keep track of all the moving parts of 196 sonnets to make sure that the lines consistently link together and ensuring the mastersonnets make coherent sense. The second challenge is that 196 is a LOT of sonnets to write. Most poets don't write that many in their entire lives (Shakespeare only wrote 154 sonnets in total), so it can be a daunting task for anyone to even consider beginning. Third, while it is easy to find a topic to write a single sonnet about, or even write a set of fourteen sonnets about, writing 196 unique sonnets all on the same subject can be almost impossible to do without getting very, very repetitive.

How did you overcome these challenges?

The first one is easy. Instead of writing on paper or using a word processor, I write in a spreadsheet where each cell represents one syllable. The cells are interlinked where they need to be so a change in one place gets carried through to all the other places.
Regarding the challenge of it being a long and daunting task, I have the preternatural ability to stubbornly complete long, repetitive projects without giving up. My first book of sonnets contained 160 sonnets specifically because I wanted to outdo the 154 sonnets in Shakespeare's oeuvre (in quantity if not in quality). So I was probably one of the few individuals who wasn't put off by the idea of spending so

much time on a single project like this (especially a project with zero commercial viability).

Regarding the third challenge of avoiding repetition, my sonnets are a bit different than the traditional sonnet. Historically, sonnets are supposed to praise something: a virtuous girl, a beautiful flower, a particularly well-written book of sonnets, etc. But that gets repetitive and boring after a dozen. My sonnets tend to be more like short stories written in sonnet form. That's not completely unheard of; for example, Shelley's *Ozymandias* is a short story in sonnet form. And honestly, wasn't the original purpose of poetry to tell stories (i.e. *Illiad, Epic of Gilgamesh, Beowulf*)? I've heard it said that, tonally, these poems are very reminiscent of the conversational form Lord Byron used in his classic epic poem, *Don Juan*. Now, admittedly, I'm the person who said that, so take it with a grain of salt.

How did you pick a topic for this crown of crowns?

It made sense to me that if one were to write a crown of crowns, the easiest way would be to find a story that could be told in fourteen different episodes and then break each of those episodes into fourteen chapters. My first idea was to retell Chaucer's *Canterbury Tales*, where each pilgrim's tale would be retold in a separate crown. But much of Chaucer's work has been lost, or is incomplete, or is borderline incoherent. My next idea was to retell the King Arthur quest for the Holy Grail, where each crown would follow the adventure of a different knight (which is basically what *Monty Python* did in their movie). But, honestly, as an intellectual property, King Arthur has already been retold a million times in a million different ways and it seemed tedious to me to go over the same ground that has already been trod again and again.

Eventually I settled on Commedia dell'Arte for a few reasons. Mainly because there is a large body of stories available to adapt, but also because the stories are mostly forgotten by modern audiences and haven't already been retold again and again. Also, the Commedia stories are designed to be improvisational and encouraging of new interpretations and, finally, it's an art form that originated in the same place (Italy) and the same time (~1500s) as sonnets originated, so there is a natural, historical connection between the two.

WHAT IS COMMEDIA DELL'ARTE?

It's a type of improvisational theater that started (probably) in Venice in the 1400s or 1500s. The general idea is that there are certain "stock characters" that the audience would be familiar with. Each character would be easily identifiable by their specific mask, costume, and mannerisms. The characters of the commedia are exaggerated versions of fixed social types: foolish old men, devious servants, star-crossed lovers, military officers full of false bravado, etc. For example, a know-it-all doctor called il Dottore Gratiano, a wealthy but oblivious old man called Pantalone, or a pair of star-crossed lovers generically known as the *Innamorati*.

While the characters were stock, their interrelationships were fluid. So, a pair could be parent and child in one scenario, business partners in the next, and romantic rivals in the scenario after that. Best not to think about it too hard. Imagine the Marx Brothers. Groucho, Chico, and Harpo are always cast as the same personality, but each role is not quite the exact same person. Sometimes they are related, sometimes just friends, sometimes coworkers, sometimes they don't know each other at all. But you know Groucho is always going to Groucho and Harpo is always going to Harpo.

Commedia performances were not scripted. The actors would be given a very general plot outline (called a scenario) and would go on stage and perform what we now call 'improv' based on the scenario and the well-known mannerisms of their stock character.

There are a few common characteristics to a Commedia performance. The characters tend to be overexaggerated versions of stereotypes. The performance has to be funny and full of witty jokes, physical humor, and slapstick (called *lazzi*). The plots all focus on love or trickery or both. It has to be bawdy and risqué (at least by the prudish standards of the 1500s). And the lower-class characters have to always outwit and embarrass the upper-class characters.

In the Middle Ages, there were a lot of traveling companies that would go around from city to city to put on Commedia shows. Every company was a bit different. Sometimes they performed one of several famous, universally-known scenarios, and sometimes they would perform a more unique, proprietary scenario. The scenarios would often be passed around between companies and adapted and reworked over and over again. Half the fun for the audience would be to see how a particular company interpreted a well-known scenario.

WHO WAS FLAMINIO SCALA?

Scala was a stage actor and producer born in 1552 in Rome, Italy. He was a pretty famous Commedia performer in his day (he was well known for playing Flavio in particular). He also wrote down a bunch of scenarios for his company to perform.

In 1611, Scala published the first collection of Scenarios of the Commedia dell'Arte, under the title *Il Teatro delle Favole Rappresentative* (A Theatrical Repertory of Fables). It contained 50 scenarios and was intended to be used as a handbook by other companies in need of inspiration and source material.

Scala's work isn't the only surviving collection of Commedia scenarios, but it is one of the earliest and best-known historical collections.

I'M A BIG, NITPICKY NERD AND THESE SONNETS HAVE MINOR DIFFERENCES FROM SCALA'S ORIGINAL STORIES.

Yes. Since Commedia is improv, it is expected that each company will exercise a lot of flexibility in how to perform each scenario. Scala's scenarios were written as full-length performances, and they contain a lot of subplots to give more actors more things to do, as well as to pad the run time. Commedia troupes would often cut them down based on time limitations and how many actors they had available. The scenarios have always been meant to be adapted and modified and passed around amongst different companies. In the introduction to his book, Scala himself wrote:

> "When I composed these works which now come into your hands, I did not think of offering them to the world in any form other than the one in which they were presented many times in the public theater. Though they have been put to work for me in this form only in the practice of my profession as an actor, and for no other purpose, the demands of patrons, the exhortations of friends, and the pleas of the curious brought me to the decision to have them printed. Afterwards, I felt I would be amply repaid, knowing that in this way there would be many more opportunities for anyone to procure my works, as I know that they have been often performed on the stage from these dramatic outlines, either in the manner offered here or in some way altered or varied."

Clearly, because a handful of sonnets can't possibly introduce every minor character and cover every subplot in an hour-long stage production, adaptations had to be made. Also...

THE CHARACTERS IN A LOT OF THESE STORIES ARE REAL JERKS AND THEY ARE UNREALISTICALLY DUMB FOR FALLING FOR THE OBVIOUS PLOT TWISTS.

Yes. The morality and artistic sensibilities of the 1500s are not the same as they are today, so a lot of the plot points in these scenarios seem a bit odd to the modern reader. And as bad as some of these characters seem in these sonnets, keep in mind that most of the really terrible things they do (like all the domestic violence and the less-than-completely-consensual sexual encounters) have been cut from these adaptations.

WHAT IS AN *INTERMEZZO*?

Commedia characters (and even the more famous actors) often were associated with specific gimmicks, skits, or bits of physical humor called *lazzi*. Sometimes the plot of the show would stop and they'd do one of these improvisational bits as a kind of intermission. If you've ever seen a Marx Brothers movie, you'll notice that in every single one, the plot grinds to a halt and Harpo plays a piece of classical music on a full-size harp that's randomly on set, regardless of how much of a non-sequitur the performance seems. But that's his *lazzo*.

In order to replicate the feel of a Commedia performance, the entirety of Crown Seven of this collection is a series of traditional *lazzi* culled from elsewhere in the historical record. Since these don't come directly from Scala's writings (as they were never written directly into the script), I decided to use a number of very popular Commedia characters that Scala didn't reference in his work (because they were invented much later), just to give them a chance to be included. That's why a lot of new names appear.

WHERE DID THE ART COME FROM?

All of the engravings contained in this book were originally published in the seminal Commedia compendium entitled, *Masques et. Buffons*, written and illustrated by Maurice Sand in 1860, which is now in the public domain.

WHAT CAN READERS EXPECT FROM THIS COLLECTION?

This book offers more than just an exercise in poetic technique—it's a journey through stories that are by turns comedic, tragic, absurd, and absolutely not profound. As you read, you'll meet a cast of characters who are as vibrant today as they were in the improvisational theaters of Renaissance Italy. Each crown offers a self-contained narrative, while the larger structure of the collection weaves these narratives into a greater whole. And, like a well-performed Commedia play, this collection promises not to take itself seriously. There's wit, humor, and even a few surprises hidden in its folds.

Finally, writing this book was a labor of love—emphasis on both "labor" and "love." It required months of revising, countless cups of coffee, and more late nights than I care to admit. But the reward of seeing these sonnets come to life in this compilation, line by line and crown by crown, made all those eyerolls from my wife worthwhile. My hope is that this collection invites you not only to enjoy these stories and characters but also to appreciate the art of formal poetry and the enduring charm of the Commedia dell'Arte.

Whether you are a lover of formalist poetry, a Italian Renaissance theater, or simply curious about the quirks of literary tradition, I welcome you to this cycle of sonnets. May you find joy in these pages and discover your own favorite moments along the way.

IL
TEATRO
delle Fauole rappresentatiue,

OVERO

LA RICREATIONE
Comica, Boscareccia, e Tragica :

DIVISA IN CINQVANTA GIORNATE,

Composte da Flaminio Scala detto Flauio Comico
del Sereniss. Sig. Duca di Mantoua.

ALL'ILL. SIG. CONTE FERDINANDO RIARIO
Marchese di Castiglione di Vald'Orcia, & Senatore in Bologna.

IN VENETIA, Appresso Gio. Battista Pulciani. M DC XI.
Con licenza de' Superiori, & Priuilegio.

Title Page from the 1611 printing
of *Il Teatro delle Favole Rappresentative*

Sonnets *of the* Commedia dell'Arte

PANTALONE

Crown No. 1:

"The Jealous Old Man"

No one will learn a lesson here today.
You'll receive no more than entertainment.
No dashing poet to make you crow "Yea!"
Just a bard... suffering from derangement.

No virtuous players; just those full of sins.
Not much moral, plot, or oratory.
In medieval Venice our tale begins –
1610, the year of our story.

Who is up first? Who is first on the stage?
'*The Jealous Old Man*' (or so Scala writes).
He quivers as he stands, stooped with old age.
Got rich profiting from famines and blights.

A man, in fine robes, though smelling of mold.
Dull Pantaloon, the miser, hordes his gold.

1.2: In which a husband and wife are introduced.

Dull Pantaloon, the miser, hordes his gold.
In Venice, he is well-known as a creep.
His wealth tremendous (or so I am told).
Yet with his ducati, he is oft' cheap.

Through extreme wealth, Pantaloon finds his pride.
...Though clinking of coins makes a hollow sound.
For he, with treasures stacked on every side,
is denied Isabelle's true love profound.

'Cause Isabelle, with eyes fresh as morning dew,
overflows with youth's beauty, poise, and grace.
A trophy wife, still yearning for love true
(or some furtive lust in this somber place).

A maiden who can sense naught but decay,
his trophy wife, Isabelle, young and gay.

1.3: In which a romantic rival is introduced.

His trophy wife, Isabelle, young and gay,
all day reads romances that make her steam.
Within her sinful heart, she longs to stray
and manifest her secret, lustful dream.

Her old man, Pantaloon, though rich and grand,
is but a shadow of the stud she seeks.
His wealth doesn't warm his cold, calloused hand
which binds her in its grasp (though it is weak).

Oratio's the one who set her heart aflame,
stirring her soul with whispers, soft and sweet.
Pantaloon smells weird; he's boring and lame.
Oratio is the man she longs to meet!

When her favors, she began to withhold,
the miser took her to a place more... controlled.

1.4: IN WHICH THE PLAYERS HEAD TO THE COUNTRYSIDE.

The miser took her to a place more controlled,
to shield his wife Isabelle from the flame
of Oratio, whom she had oft' extolled.
Pantaloon hoped she'd forget that guy's name.

In his country house, surrounded by green,
the miser would safeguard his cherished prize.
Yet even here, where she remained unseen,
her husband's constraints, Isabelle defies.

Pedro, the servant and malicious kid,
bore witness to Isabelle's wistful moans,
and in his mind a cunning plan was bid
to, at Pantaloon's ego, throw some stones.

And as he stroked his chin full of stubble,
Pedro the servant schemed to make trouble.

1.5: In which a servant oversteps his station.

Pedro the servant schemed to make trouble.
His mind focused on mischief's dark delight.
Told Oratio to his efforts redouble
and seek Isabelle the very next night.

"Nearby is the estate of Pantaloon,"
he whispered low with a gleam in his eyes.
"If you leave right now, you'll get there quite soon...
Where Isabelle waits beneath starry skies."

"Not too far from there – really quite close by...
I've secured a romantic, hidden place...
Near Pantaloon's villa, as the crows fly...
is where you'll enjoy Isabelle's embrace!"

"For I've heard rumor there will be a ball...
a party held by Tino and Pasquale."

1.6: In which an invitation arrives.

A party, held by Tino and Pasquale!
There'll be festive music! Maybe she'll dance?
A change from routine boring and banal
might rekindle his and his bride's romance?

Pantaloon won't this invitation spurn,
'cause the miser hopes love will find a way.
While in Isabelle's loins, passion doth yearn.
From her conjugal bed, she longs to stray.

So within Tino and Pasquale's merry hall,
where hoi polloi dance in the candlelight,
she'll seek a new meaning to the word... *ball*.
Passions will bloom under cover of night.

For Pedro knows a place, dark and subtle;
just the spot for a rendezvous-double...

1.7: In which another conspirator conspires.

Just the spot for a rendezvous-double,
Pasquale's chambers provide the perfect scene.
Pedro and Pasquale had built a bubble
where lovers could sin and get away clean.

Pasquale, with devilish grin upon her face,
ensures a room is set for two young hearts.
She agrees to provide secluded space
where Isabelle can practice bawdy arts.

The conspirators chuckle, now full of glee,
as they finalize details of their plan
to arrange a most sinful intimacy
and embarrass a prideful, bitter, old man.

After Pedro gets details from the gal,
Oratio is told of the locale.

1.8: IN WHICH ORATIO PATIENTLY AWAITS HIS LOVER.

Oratio is told of the locale.
He soon arrives randy, ready for sin.
Pasquale leads him with stealth (she's such a pal)
to the hidden chamber where he'll stick it in.

Oratio's heart no longer feels despair
in the small boudoir in which he does lie.
Anticipation instead fills the air
for soon Isabelle's form would meet his eye.

In steamy tones, the two lovers would speak
and share a moist kiss and soft tender touch.
While outside, the grand ball started to peak
and Pantaloon stayed... unaware of much.

Soon, all was prepared and right on cue;
Isabelle asked her hosts to use the loo.

1.9: In which Isabelle excuses herself.

Isabelle asked her hosts to use the loo.
She awkwardly claimed she'd drank too much beer.
And with a loud, feigned burp, she slipped from view
while Pantaloon exclaimed, "Hurry back, dear."

She sought not the privy, but Pasquale's lair.
To finally hold a man in his prime!
So crazed with consummating the affair,
the lovers too loudly enjoyed their playtime.

Pantaloon, naïve to the cause of her moans,
assumed Isabelle really had to go.
While locked away, she boisterously bones
(and bones and bones) her lover Oratio.

Worried a guest would intrude on her chore,
jealous Pantaloon guards the bathroom door.

1.10: In which Pantaloon attempts gallantry.

Jealous Pantaloon guards the bathroom door
to shield his wife from prying eyes and jest.
Stands guard like a knight in the Captain's corps
to ensure Isabelle's moment of rest.

He fears intrusion while she's on the can.
Desiring her modesty might be kept,
he doesn't realize that she's with a man;
his dear Isabelle is with passion swept.

As Pantaloon remained unaware,
they coupled five times, thirst undiminished.
Once fully spent, they embrace once with care;
Isabelle exits... now that she's finished.

And Pantaloon noticed a... rosy hue
when Isabelle returned after her screw.

I.II: In which Pantaloon remains oblivious.

When Isabelle returned after her screw,
Pantaloon took his dear wife's hand with care.
He thought her absence was just for the loo;
never considered her heated affair.

Her hair all a mess, sweat dripped from her brow;
obvious by the way she walked gaited,
she'd recently betrayed her wedding vow.
Isabelle's passion had just been sated.

He gave her advice that took her aback,
mistaking her cries for gastric distress.
"When the feeling comes over you, don't hold back
because nature's call cannot be suppressed!"

All of the guests – including the server –
all but Pantaloon could now see love's fervor.

1.12: In which the truth is revealed to Pantaloon.

All but Pantaloon could now see love's fervor,
as whispers spread through halls like a geyser.
Pedro and Tino (a neutral observer)
revealed the harsh truth to the old miser.

"My dear Master," Pedro told him with care,
"Your wife's affair is known to all but you."
Tino adds, "You can see it in the air...
She's been unfaithful; no doubt that is true!"

The weight of words drops heavy on his chest.
A revelation sharp as winter's chill.
His trust now shattered; he's shocked and depressed
(since infidelity is a bitter pill).

And as Pantaloon feels his heart grow cold,
Oratio makes an accusation bold.

1.13: In which Oratio makes a startling accusation.

Oratio makes an accusation bold,
with fiery gaze and words both sharp and keen.
He claimed that Pantaloon is far too old
and had left Isabelle's virtues... unseen.

"To all assembled here," he loudly states,
"Your Isabelle was pure before my eyes...
Her sweet maidenhood had not met its fate...
Her heart and body knew no prior ties."

"And Isabelle... Your husband's aged and weak...
His strength too feeble, your desires denied...
He never gave you the thing that you seek...
You were still a virgin. And that's bona-fide!"

'Twas plainly quite clear, throughout the household,
on stage are two lovers and a cuckold.

1.14: In which Pantaloon accepts his sorry fate.

On stage are two lovers and a cuckold.
Pantaloon stands with heart feeling squeezed.
He faced that hard truth, let his defense fold;
admitted his wife had never been pleased.

"Indeed," he spoke, "My strength has waned with age...
And I have failed to meet her carnal needs...
If Oratio can her wild passions cage...
Let him claim her hand while mine will recede."

With weary grace he opens wide the door
to Isabelle and Oratio's embrace.
The old man's wealth's no match for a love pure,
and he must find solace in his disgrace.

In letting go, he took the humble way
and Pantaloon learned a lesson that day.

I: MASTERSONNET:

No one will learn a lesson here today.
Dull Pantaloon, the miser, hordes his gold.
His trophy wife Isabelle, young and gay.
The miser took her to a place more controlled.

Pedro the servant, schemed to make trouble.
A party held by Tino and Pasquale,
just the spot for a rendezvous-double.
Oratio is told of the locale.

Isabelle asked her hosts to use the loo.
Jealous Pantaloon guards the bathroom door.
When Isabelle returned after her screw,
all but Pantaloon could see love's fervor.

Oratio makes an accusation bold –
On stage are two lovers and a cuckold.

FLAVIO

Crown No. 2:

"Flavio Betrayed"

2.1: IN WHICH THE MAIN CHARACTER IS INTRODUCED.

On stage are two lovers and a cuckold.
(Though things may not be quite as they appear...)
In Pisa, is where these events unfold;
1610 is the approximate year.

This play was named '*Flavio Betrayed*'.
It's about Flavio (as you might guess).
His friend's a rake who just wants to get laid,
and that guy ends up making quite a mess.

This is not high drama, tragedy Greek –
just filthy comedy penned by a bard.
Not a work of philosophy antique
so try not to read into it too hard.

Let's start and end in the time allotted...
Flavio and Isabelle are besotted.

2.2: IN WHICH TWO LOVERS YEARN FOR THEIR WEDDING DAY.

Flavio and Isabelle are besotted.
(Besotted's a word that means they're attracted.)
All around town they were often spotted
whispering suggestively 'bout [REDACTED].

They hoped that quite soon down the aisle they'd walk.
Desperate they were to get married post-haste.
You see, despite all their amorous talk,
they'd not even kissed. Their love was quite chaste.

Isabelle wanted to wait 'til marriage
before she would make the beast with two backs.
Flavio would not her virtue disparage
and so he'd just have to wait to climax.

One day, about his frustration he told
his 'friend' Oratio (a knave brash and bold).

2.3: In which Flavio confides in the wrong person.

His 'friend' Oratio (a knave brash and bold)
just happened to also crave Isabelle.
A scoundrel with no honor to uphold,
under her untouched skirts, he sought to dwell.

But, Oratio acted proper and prim,
so Flavio remained oblivious.
He thought his friend would be happy for him.
No inkling the rogue was lascivious.

"How can I sway her father Dottore...
to agree to give me Isabelle's hand?"
He hoped his friend would offer oratory,
but Oratio had another thing planned.

Naïve Flavio, he should have spotted
a bitter rival with schemes quite knotted.

2.4: In which a second romantic rival briefly appears.

A bitter rival with schemes quite knotted.
Of course, that knave would have to get in line...
For Dottore had already spotted
a potential match with the right bloodline.

The Captain had fame, fortune, and money.
Just the right features to make a good groom.
So what if he smelled a little funny?
With his bank account, love was sure to bloom.

"Isabelle, I've made the Captain an offer...
I can see you're too excited to speak...
He's very eager to fill your *coffer*...
The wedding is set for early next week!"

Not content to spend her life with that boor,
Isabelle writes pleas to her paramour.

2.5: In which Isabelle pens a desperate love letter.

Isabelle writes pleas to her paramour.
On scented paper, she pens a letter.
But how to get it to Flavio's door?
She'd need lots of aid from an abettor...

But who could she find that would be fervent?
Could not be entrusted to just any punk.
The only one here was Pedro the servant
(and that moron was an infamous drunk).

But, desperate times call for desperate measure.
She had no choice, so in spite of herself,
entrusted him with her precious treasure
which the drunken fool promptly left on a shelf.

And while Pedro loafed in good humor,
Flavio's discouraged by a rumor.

2.6: In which Flavio receives some alarming news.

Flavio's discouraged by a rumor.
Overheard something he wasn't suspecting.
Would rather have learned he had a tumor
than find out Isabelle was *expecting*...

As he and Oratio strolled through the square,
the two crossed Isabelle's friend Columbine.
She gave Oratio an ominous stare,
called him a pig and a cad and a swine!

"How dare you take advantage of my friend...
Luring her into your carnal pleasure...
Her maidenhood has met its gruesome end...
Her belly grows big with your foul *treasure*."

The news makes Flavio fall on the floor,
But Oratio's second bombshell's in store...

2.7: In which Oratio makes a bold proposition.

But Oratio's second bombshell's in store
as Flavio slinks off to lick his wounds.
The scoundrel appears at Dottore's door,
flowers in hand, with his tunic festooned.

"I've come here today dressed in fancy clothes...
carrying presents and this ring made of pearl...
While I'm poor and crass and have a large nose...
I've come to propose to your little girl."

"To the Captain, I can't hold a candle...
Even so, Isabelle has to be mine...
If you don't agree, there will be scandal...
She carries my child – go ask Columbine!"

Confronted by this daring presumer,
her dad Dottore's not in good humor.

2.8: IN WHICH DOTTORE FINDS SOME PROOF.

Her dad Dottore's not in good humor.
He throws Oratio out by his britches.
Then bellows and hollers (what a boomer),
mourning the loss of his chance at riches.

"Could it be a lie?" He thinks to himself.
No proof yet it's true, it's not bona-fide.
But then he spies the note left on the shelf
and soon his suspicions are verified.

Written in her hand, addressed to 'My Beau',
"Please take me away, it's you I adore!"
Who it's written to, it does not say so
...though who but Oratio could it be for?

His daughter's deed means he'll still be a debtor.
Dottore confronts her about the letter.

2.9: In which Dottore confronts his daughter.

Dottore confronts her about the letter
as she's in the kitchen eating a crumpet.
While her lip quivers and her eyes get wetter,
he accuses her of being a strumpet.

Dottore asks why she chose such a lout,
but naïve Isabelle never realizes
it's not Flavio he's talking about,
but vile Oratio (a man she despises).

"It's true, Dad. I love him!" She shouts and screams,
"I'll never wed the Captain, he's old and gross...
I'm already with the man of my dreams...
And if I can't have him, I'll just overdose!"

Plot twist – Oratio she never did screw.
Pedro finds out that the rumor's untrue.

2.10: In which a humble servant learns the truth.

Pedro finds out that the rumor's untrue
while in the town square with a jug of wine.
When all of a sudden, who should walk through
but his former love interest Columbine.

"You're looking quite well," he says to his flame.
"Is that a new dress? How'd you get so flush?"
"Pedro," she says, "I see you're still drunk and lame...
I will tell you, but it's secret, so shush..."

"Some chump offered to pay fifty scudi...
If I just walked up to him on the street...
And told him right in front of his buddy...
That everyone knew Isabelle did cheat."

Still remorseful for losing the letter,
the servant seeks to make it all better.

2.11: In which Pedro reveals what he's learned.

The servant seeks to make it all better
and get back in Isabelle's good graces.
First, he thinks he could knit her a sweater...
No, that's dumb; she wants Flavio's embraces.

He searches the town for the jilted boyfriend
and finds him climbing on a bridge's rail.
"Flavio! No need for your life to end...
Your love isn't pregnant – 'tis just a tale!"

"You have no idea how much this has weighed...
On my mind," Flavio says climbing down.
But he can't believe how he's been betrayed.
She was faithful... that Oratio's a clown.

Since no one has told him it isn't true,
the Captain, though, is still feeling quite blue.

2.12: In which the Captain swears vengeance.

The Captain, though, is still feeling quite blue
after speaking to his ex-father-in-law.
"Captain, I'm sorry, but there's been a coup...
And Isabelle's hand I'll have to withdraw."

Dottore is embarrassed to admit
Isabelle is no longer a virgin.
Some baby booties, she will have to knit
for in her belly, a child doth burgeon.

In a few months, she will enter labor
and Oratio's son will spill from her womb.
The hot-headed Captain grabs his saber
and vows to send the rascal to his tomb.

He's quite upset that his bride went astray
so it's Oratio that he seeks to slay.

2.13: In which Oratio's life is endangered.

While it's Oratio that he seeks to slay,
first, the Captain stops to sharpen his blade.
Then he'll kill anyone who gets in the way
(after all, battle has long been his trade).

He finds the knave drunk in a seedy bar.
By his tunic, drags him out on the street.
"Ready yourself, boy, we're going to spar!"
Oratio's bowels begin to excrete.

The Captain won't just stab him in the face.
Not gonna rush – take his time, make it slow.
Oratio pleads for his life, in disgrace,
when Flavio appears, armed with crossbow.

Fret not, dear reader – no one will die today –
it's only commedia dell'arte!

2.14: In which the plot of the story is resolved.

It's only commedia dell'arte!
So you know this story must end light.
It's not drama – 'tis a comedic play.
Let's zip ahead to the end of the fight...

The Captain ran off in a cloud of dust.
(T'was not a brave fighter, just a poseur.)
Flavio says, "Friend, you betrayed my trust...
But I can't let you just die like a cur."

Oratio's moved and admits his deceit.
"This awful prank I'm sorry I began...
Your bride's honor's intact – she did not cheat!
Marry her today; I'll be your best man!"

Curtain closes on a ribald play of old.
On stage are two lovers, but no cuckold.

2: MASTERSONNET.

On stage are two lovers and a cuckold.
Flavio and Isabelle are besotted.
His 'friend' Oratio (a knave brash and bold) –
A bitter rival... with schemes quite knotted.

Isabelle writes pleas to her paramour.
Flavio's discouraged by a rumor.
But Oratio's second bombshell's in store.
Her dad Dottore's not in good humor.

Dottore confronts her about the letter.
Pedro finds out that the rumor's untrue.
The servant seeks to make it all better.
The Captain, though, is still feeling quite blue.

While it's Oratio that he vows to slay –
It's only commedia dell'arte!

FLAMINA

Crown No. 3:

"The Betrothed"

3.1: In which the scenario is introduced.

It's only commedia dell'arte!
Expect something funny, not dramatic.
Plays that are oft' 'bout lovers led astray
with plot twists confusing and erratic.

Suitors and maidens scheme throughout Venice.
But partners get dumped ('cause love is fickle).
Scorned Isabelle turns into a menace
and leaves some wedding guests in a pickle.

'*The Betrothed*' is this tale written by Scala,
a bard and Renaissance playwright of note.
Who was born in Rome (not Guatemala)
and famous enough for Shakespeare to quote.

The curtain rises, 1610 is the date –
An antique tale of love, passion, and hate.

3.2: In which two lovers are betrothed.

An antique tale of love, passion, and hate
begins with sweet Oratio pitching woo.
Declaring his love, he intends to date
the buxom Isabelle who loved him too.

But back then couples could not just have sex.
That would be a sin (they lived near the Pope).
They'd first have to wed, and if dad objects,
it was decided they would just elope.

"Let's not ask your dad yet," says Isabelle,
"Pantaloon's busy with lots on his plate."
His days filled with importing goods to sell
and also finding his servant a mate.

Arranging him a bride, hale and hearty,
Pantaloon plans Pedro's wedding party.

3.3: In which Pantaloon arranges a marriage for his servant.

Pantaloon plans Pedro's wedding party.
"Pedro, my boy," Pantaloon says with a grin,
"You've earned lots of coin; you're quite a smarty...
But never found a bride, to your chagrin...

"You're quite ugly; not in anyone's league...
But lucky for you, I have something planned...
In Padua, I have a colleague...
He has a daughter who needs a husband...

"On your behalf, I've made an arrangement...
I've not seen her yet; I'm told that she's fine...
Say you'll be true. Promise no estrangement...
And you can wed the lovely Columbine."

But while letters are sent to "Save the Date,"
jealous Flamina schemes Oratio's fate.

3.4: In which Flamina steals a groom for herself.

Jealous Flamina schemes Oratio's fate.
Though just as comely as was her rival,
her dowry's meager – just one small estate.
Finding a rich groom was just plain survival.

"Dottore... Father...," she asks with a smile.
"I hear Oratio is very single...
His father, Pantaloon, has quite the *stockpile*...
Perhaps you could help arrange a... mingle?"

Dottore and Pantaloon oft' played poker,
and deals were often struck 'round the table.
A marriage agreement they did broker.
Kids betrothed to wed, soon as they're able.

While, "I'll kill that bitch!" Isabelle was screaming,
other scorned lovers were also steaming...

3.5: In which three scorned lovers swear vengeance.

Other scorned lovers were also steaming.
Sure, Isabelle has lost her honeybun.
But her brother, Spaventa, who'd been dreaming
of wedding Flamina is also done.

And, too, Isabelle's servant Harlequin,
who had hoped to make Columbine his wife.
That romance now had no chance to begin.
Pedro, that big jerk, had ruined his life!

Three true loves lost, three lovers dejected.
In each other they would commiserate.
They refused to have their needs neglected.
Each swore revenge; vowed to retaliate.

A plan is hatched for three days from today...
As Pedro's grand wedding gets underway.

3.6: In which a grand wedding is held.

As Pedro's grand wedding gets underway,
guests arrive from all over the region.
From Milan, to Naples, and even Cathay;
none want to miss the event of the season.

Fine foods piled high, Pantaloon beams with pride,
flaunting copious wealth for all to see.
Pedro paced, fretting – he has not seen the bride
and he wonders how wedded life will be.

The three scorned lovers sneak in in disguise,
each dressed in the plain garb of a waiter.
In their minds, each lover plans the demise
of the rival they considered a traitor.

Soon comes a sight to make guests think they're dreaming;
Flamina, chased by Isabelle, screaming.

3.7: In which a violent duel interrupts the ceremony.

Flamina's chased by Isabelle, screaming
and swinging a rapier 'cross the ballroom.
"By my sword, soon your blood will be streaming...
Flamina, you harlot! You stole by groom!"

Flamina blocks blows with a chafing dish.
She's not ready yet to give up the ghost.
"Dying here today was never my wish...
I only wanted to notch my bedpost!"

Flamina was jealous of her rival's luck.
Never fancied Oratio... in specific.
But she had no beau – not even a schmuck
so stealing her rival's man seemed terrific.

And while Flamina likely gets away,
t'was not the only violence that day.

3.8: In which a second duel occurs.

T'was not the only violence that day.
Oratio was also running scared
out the front door, followed without delay,
by an angry Spaventa, nostrils' flared.

"Spaventa, I beg, you've made a mistake...
Flamina, though comely, isn't my type...
Isabelle's the one who makes my heart ache...
Your paramour, I'm not trying to swipe...

"Instead, blame my father, Pantaloon...
And Flamina's father Dottore, too...
As matchmakers go, they are but buffoons...
Never asked if I wanted to say, 'I do.'"

While Oratio 'cross the courtyard, careens,
Isabelle's leal servant spills all the beans.

3.9: In which a servant makes a shocking accusation.

Isabelle's leal servant spills all the beans;
tells both fathers Isabelle's honest truth.
She's fancied Oratio since they were teens.
Love at first sight, betrothed since their youth.

Harlequin says that he's all but certain
that the two lovers had had... carnal fun.
He once caught them hiding 'neath a curtain
and noticed Oratio's britches undone.

"Oh my!" Pantaloon says, "Now things have changed...
My son Oratio must honor his vow...
A wedding to Isabelle must be arranged...
Dottore, I'll make this up to you somehow."

Dottore nods because it's understood.
No spouse would be satisfied with used goods.

3.10: In which a new betrothal is quickly negotiated.

No spouse would be satisfied with used goods.
Flamina won't want Oratio's soiled hand.
The betrothal was off after these falsehoods.
But, in that case, something else must be planned.

He asks, "Is there an alternate she could meet?"
"What about that furious chap with the sword?"
"The one chasing Oratio down the street?"
"With a man like that, she'd never get bored."

"Good point," says the sly merchant Pantaloon.
"And assuming he doesn't first kill my son...
I'm willing to pay for the whole honeymoon."
They agreed and shook hands, "This deal is done!"

Two rich old cronies work behind the scenes
and Spaventa finds love through other means.

3.11: IN WHICH SPAVENTA FINALLY DECLARES HIS LOVE.

And Spaventa finds love through other means,
even as Oratio did soon escape.
Spaventa's sword swipe almost got him clean,
but he missed, and then tripped over his cape.

Flamina, avoiding Isabelle's wrath
by hiding 'til Isabelle was done venting,
spies Spaventa sitting on the path.
His rage is now spent; he's just lamenting.

Eye-to-eye, he works up the courage to say,
"For so long now, I've loved you from afar."
They return hand-in-hand to the soiree;
after all, there's food and an open bar.

As Flamina's lonely heart throbs (as it should),
a surprising guest comes out of the wood.

3.12: IN WHICH PEDRO MEETS AN UNEXPECTED GUEST.

A surprising guest comes out of the wood
(who we'll circle back to in a sec...).
Pedro meanwhile searched as hard as he could;
can't find Columbine to give her a peck.

He lost her somewhere in the disorder.
Maybe she ran away with another?
By now, she might be halfway to the border.
"Could sure use the help of Tino, my brother!"

"Who calls me?" said Tino, the surprising guest.
Pedro asks why he's here, hands him some wine.
Tino explains, "I came at the bequest...
Of my daughter, the bride Columbine."

The look on his face – a sight to behold.
His wedding vow, Pedro's forced to withhold.

3.13: In which an inappropriate betrothal is withdrawn.

His wedding vow, Pedro's forced to withhold.
He'd not seen his estranged brother in years.
Pedro did not know, had never been told,
Tino had married and this child was theirs.

"I can't believe Columbine... is my niece?!?"
This solemn occasion becomes a farce.
"Can't marry her now; they'd call the police!"
Pantaloon, laughs, "Seems you're out on your arse!"

Harlequin appears, steps up to the plate.
"Pantaloon, don't let this ball go to waste...
I love Columbine and we want to mate...
Since you paid for the priest, wed us post-haste!"

The priest changed his draft, took Pantaloon's gold,
improvising off a script that's quite old.

3.14: In which not one, but three weddings are held.

Improvising off a script that's quite old,
the priest scribbles down his new wedding speech.
Wasn't prepared for nuptials three-fold,
as two other couples rose to beseech.

Harlequin and Columbine tied the knot.
Spaventa and Flamina walked the aisle.
Isabelle's bouquet, some maiden soon caught.
Dottore and Pantaloon both did smile.

Forlorn Pedro remained the odd man out,
the only groom who was left in the cold.
He'd one day find love without a doubt
But that's a different tale to be told...

Please keep in mind as we end this party:
t'was only commedia dell'arte!

3: MASTERSONNET.

It's only commedia dell'arte,
An antique tale of love, passion, and hate.
Pantaloon plans Pedro's wedding party.
Jealous Flamina schemes Oratio's fate.

Other scorned lovers are also steaming,
as Pedro's grand wedding gets underway.
Flamina's chased by Isabelle, screaming.
T'was not the only violence that day.

Isabelle's leal servant spills all the beans.
No bride would be satisfied with used goods.
And Spaventa finds love through other means.
A surprising guest comes out of the woods.

His wedding vow, Pedro's forced to withhold,
adapting a tale from a script that's quite old.

ISABELLA

Crown No. 4:

"Isabella's Trick"

4.1: IN WHICH SOME CHARACTER NAMES ARE CLARIFIED.

Improvising off a script that's quite old –
in fact, one written in the late medieval.
Shocked that the book hasn't succumbed to mold
or been consumed by a ravenous weevil.

'*Isabella's Trick*' is the tale I'll tell,
but four-syllable words are hard to time.
I shortened her name to just 'Isabelle.'
In an adaptation, that's not a huge crime.

Anyway... In Milan, she does a mean thing,
which stops two romances from proceeding.
So, Isabelle finds a new prank to spring
that let's everyone get back to breeding.

Do not close your eyes; you don't want to miss:
Captain's in love with Oratio's sis.

4.2: In which Captain Spaventa declares his love.

Captain's in love with Oratio's sis.
The sis in question is, of course, Isabelle.
He seeks advice from his friend about this,
"Flavio, she has me under her spell!...

"Why do I love her? Let me count the ways...
She can spin wool fine as a spider...
Her skills in the scullery? Worthy of praise!...
And her birthing hips couldn't be wider."

His friend's more concerned 'bout her attitude.
Flavio asks, "Isn't she a bit mean?"
The Captain though loves the fact she's quite rude.
"To you she's a shrew, but to me? A queen!"

Soon another twist begins to unfold;
Flavio loves Flamina's hair of gold.

4.3: In which Flavio declares his love.

Flavio loves Flamina's hair of gold.
(Note: the Captain is Flamina's brother.)
"Her lips, I long to kiss; her hand, to hold...
Bet your sister would make a great mother...

"The glow of her skin, the smell of her hair...
The fit of her bustle couldn't be better...
Not to mention her ample derriere...
Please agree to pass her this love letter?"

"You have a good job; your shoulders are broad...
On her loveliness, I see how you dote...
Flavio! Let us get brother-in-lawed...
I'd be most glad to deliver your note."

And so, together, friends plan wedded bliss.
No cause to believe anything's amiss.

4.4: In which a letter is warmly received.

No cause to believe anything's amiss.
The letter is sent, and a week later,
Flavio, with roses and chocolates Swiss,
knocks on Flamina's front door to date her.

She invites him in, accepts his presents.
She's always found her brother's friend dreamy.
They discuss Flavio's letter's contents
(which I won't describe here, as it's quite steamy).

Flamina's been waiting for Flavio.
"I admit that your proposal made me blush...
If you're asking if you can be my beau...
My answer is yes! I will be your crush."

Talk ensues so sappy, it'd make you sick,
though jokers can't resist playing a trick.

4.5: In which a jape is played to catastrophic result.

Though jokers can't resist playing a trick,
sometimes there's serious consequences.
And Isabelle's not slightly politic –
in fact, she relishes causing offenses.

When Flavio asks what Isabelle thinks
regarding dear Flamina's true feelings,
Isabelle can't resist a lie that stinks
to set innocent Flavio reeling.

"Hate to tell you... the Captain's plans have changed...
He's betrothed Flamina to Oratio...
Don't know what to say. It's all been arranged
so I can wed the Captain, quid pro quo."

Isn't concerned 'bout the lie she's just spun.
"Just a jape," thinks Isabelle, having fun.

4.6: In which Isabelle makes things significantly worse.

"Just a jape," thinks Isabelle, having fun.
Since it worked once, might as well double-down.
The look on their faces when I am done.
"Oh boy," she says, "I'm a riotous clown!"

"Hey, Flamina," she shouts to her neighbor,
"I hear to Oratio you're now engaged...
He'll be here soon to present his *saber*...
T'was Captain's doing. Hope you're not enraged."

"No way my brother would do such a thing?!?"
"I do pinky swear, he can and he did...
So Oratio'd let him give me a ring."
Flamina cries, "I'll run off to Madrid!"

As Isabelle goes home, laughs herself sick,
Flavio confronts Flamina real quick.

4.7: In which Pantaloon makes an unwelcomed appearance.

Flavio confronts Flamina real quick.
She's on the street searching for her brother.
Seems that both fell for Isabelle's slapstick.
"Say it's not true that you'll marry another?!?"

Flamina's mad he thinks she'd be untrue.
Flavio's mad she agreed to a switch.
Then, of course, more chaos starts to ensue
when Pantaloon steps in to make a pitch.

The miser awkwardly proposes.
Angry Flamina accepts out of spite.
Flavio storms off. His ring, he disposes.
The two lovers had a heck of a fight.

Their dreams of wedded bliss? Now they have none.
It's Isabelle's fault their bond is undone.

4.8: In which Isabelle feels regret for her jape.

It's Isabelle's fault their bond is undone.
Flamina stomps home, followed by the miser.
She calls him a clod – rather be a nun –
Slams the door in his face, cries a geyser.

He's driven off when a bucket of water
is tossed down from Isabelle's second floor.
"This prank got out of hand," thinks the plotter.
"Must do something fast to bring back ardor...

"How can I fix this? Pranks are all I know...
and apologies just aren't my style."
She paces and paces around her room, slow.
Nothing. Then nothing. But after a while...

Something as devious as it is swell!
A bawdy new prank planned by Isabelle.

4.9: IN WHICH THE PLAYERS ARE MOVED INTO POSITION.

A bawdy new prank planned by Isabelle
starts by getting all the players on stage.
Oratio is asked, "A lie can you tell?...
Just a joke to make the Captain enraged...

"Say you agree to your sister's marriage...
Then tell him I await him in our house...
He must make haste, run or take a carriage...
Go into my room, await his new spouse...

"When he arrives, the lights will be dim...
And someone awaits him in the bed...
But it won't be myself that's waiting for him...
It will be that clod Pantaloon instead!"

Oratio runs off, to the Captain surprise.
All can be fixed with a few more white lies.

4.10: In which a concupiscent suitor arrives.

All can be fixed with a few more white lies.
She told Oratio she'd find Pantaloon
and dress him up in an 'Isabelle disguise.'
She's not. The prank doesn't need that buffoon.

Instead, she hides behind the well in the yard.
Soon, Oratio arrives with his mark.
Seems he's been taken in by the canard.
"Go right on inside; I hope there's a spark!"

The Captain enters, smile on his face.
The trap set, Oratio runs off chuckling.
"The whole town will want to see us replace...
The Captain's bride with that ugly duckling."

Prank's not done just yet. She must make as well
more gullible players fall for her spell.

4.11: In which the several more lies are told.

More gullible players fall for her spell.
She crosses the street, knocks on Flamina's door.
"My dear, Oratio is feeling unwell...
In fact, the lovesick fool cried his eyes sore."

Flamina comes down, bags packed for her flight.
"Before you flee, please, he should be consoled."
Flamina replies, "I'll do it for spite...
I've been dumped! Why should my love I withhold?"

"Oratio's upstairs, first room on the left."
She guides Flamina into her villa.
This prank works because Flamina's bereft.
Too angry for doubt (not one scintilla).

One thing is left, then she'll spring the surprise.
None suspect scheming Isabelle's disguise.

4.12: IN WHICH THE THIRD SUITOR IS TRICKED.

None suspect scheming Isabelle's disguise.
Especially not Flavio, feeling blue.
She finds him at the pub, subtly implies,
"Don't want the Captain – want to marry *you*."

She says it sweetly as she takes his hand.
Flavio must admit, he's taken aback.
This certainly was not something he'd planned.
"But why not pay that wench Flamina back?"

They head to her place for a torrid affair.
"While I freshen up, inside you should go...
First room on the left, wait for me upstairs."
Into her villa, she guides Oratio.

These guys are all chumps, so easy to sway.
Manipulated as if in a ballet.

4.13: In which a crowd of townsfolk arrive.

Manipulated as if in a ballet.
Four people thought their problems were bigger,
about to have the most marvelous day.
Isabelle springs her trap, pulls the trigger.

She enters the Captain's room on the right.
On the left, the other two interacted.
It was pitch black, no one turned on the light.
Couldn't see to whom they were attracted.

Outside, townsfolk of Milan start to arrive.
Everyone came at Oratio's behest.
Some amusement they expect to derive.
Could all that moaning be part of the jest?

Four people make love with their fiancé.
They are just performers in a light play.

4.14: In which the lovers' true identities are revealed.

They are just performers in a light play.
Noticing nothing until copulation's complete.
With passion they were so carried away,
they could not hear the cheering from the street.

Two windows are opened, four faces peer out.
Naked, they look down on the crowd below.
Embarrassed, because now, without any doubt,
their deflowering was... very thorough.

"I guess we're engaged," says one couple.
"If you are, then I guess we must be, too."
All head inside to their lusting redouble.
Next day, they find a priest to say "I do."

Isabelle saved the day with the lies she told.
T'was improvised off a script that's quite old.

4: MASTERSONNET:

Improvising off a script that's quite old.
Captain's in love with Oratio's sis.
Flavio loves Flamina's hair of gold.
No cause to believe anything's a miss.

Though jokers can't resist playing a trick.
"Just a jape," thinks Isabelle, having fun.
Flavio confronts Flamina real quick.
It's Isabelle's fault their bond is undone.

A bawdy new prank planned by Isabelle.
All can be fixed with just a few white lies.
More gullible players fall for the spell.
None suspect scheming Isabelle's disguise.

Manipulated as if in a ballet.
They are just performers in a light play.

IL CAPITANO

Crown No. 5:

"The Twin Captains"

5.1: In which a set of identical twins is introduced.

They are just performers in a light play,
staged in the style "Commedia dell'art."
Sometimes, to financial concerns allay,
the same actor performs more than one part.

In this tale, the Captain does double duty.
Acting two parts does require more skill.
But don't clap too hard, lest he get snooty.
In Commedia, 'tis run of the mill.

Around 1610, he left the town of Rome.
His wife Isabelle was less than amused.
In '*The Twin Captains*', a Captain comes home,
but which one has returned? All are confused.

A wife, vs. two men born of the same mother.
A damsel, a Captain, and his twin brother.

5.2: IN WHICH A LONG JOURNEY IS UNDERTAKEN.

A damsel, a Captain, and his twin brother.
The Captain and Isabelle start off wed.
No doubt that the two loved one another,
yet one morn', the Captain jumps out of bed.

"Isabelle, my dear, I must go find my twin...
He's gone missing while off fighting the Turk...
Where I should look? Don't know where to begin...
But if I don't try, I'll feel like a jerk."

With that, the Captain packed clothes in a case,
took his sword and his cloak, kissed her goodbye.
"I'll search deserts, bogs, and even deep space...
Should return in a year... unless I die."

Isabelle waits for a year and a day.
A quick trip becomes a long time away.

5.3: In which a frustrated Isabelle seeks an
    alternative.

A quick trip becomes a long time away.
One year turns into two, two into six.
Too long since Isabelle's gotten to play.
She grows tired of not wetting her wick.

Her neighbor Flamina has a great man.
(Strong chin, broad shoulders, plenty of muscle.)
Isabelle fantasizes a lustful plan
to coax Oratio under her bustle.

In the street, she drops her handkerchief,
shows him some ankle when he picks it up.
Of course, Flamina's neither blind nor deaf,
won't stand for him filling Isabelle's cup.

Each hopes Oratio will forsake the other.
Rivals for love resent one another.

5.4: In which two romantic rivals quarrel.

Rivals for love resent one another.
Flamina confronts her, "You need to leave!"
Isabelle threatens to stab or smother.
In this war of love, there'll be no reprieve.

Isabelle's servant, Columbine, steps in.
Stands up for her master, causing a stir.
Shouts, "Flamina! You're ugly and too thin."
That arrogant wench! Flamina beats her.

Love-crazed Isabelle jumps into the fray.
Swings her milk-can right at Flamina's head.
Oratio steps betwixt and saves the day.
"You ladies must stop, or one'll end up dead."

The women all stomp from the marketplace.
Oratio has his pick of girls to chase.

5.5: In which Oratio seeks advice.

Oratio has his pick of girls to chase.
He needs Pedro for some quick consultation.
Heads to Pedro's Inn (he owns a nice place).
Asks how he could reduce confrontation.

"Oratio," Pedro says, assessing the odds,
"Flamina's cute, but Isabelle's wealthy...
You're a fine catch, better than other clods...
Pick the mate who'll keep you fat and healthy."

"Pedro," he responds, "you make a good point...
But Flamina's the one I long to hug...
Now, Isabelle's nose is all out of joint...
And as you know, she can be quite a thug."

Day after Oratio warned of danger,
Pedro spies a mysterious stranger.

5.6: In which an innkeeper spies a mysterious visitor.

Pedro spies a mysterious stranger,
who makes him shiver, goosebumps on his skin.
He'd been out back, preparing the manger,
when he returned, the man was checking in.

Rented a room, passed scudi to the clerk.
He sounds like the Captain, smelled like him, too.
"Just come back home, been off fighting the Turk!"
Pedro eavesdropped, didn't know what to do.

Doesn't bode well if the Captain's in town.
His jealousy puts Oratio at risk.
Pedro inches close, and pulls his cap down,
with a broom he gives the Inn's floor a whisk.

Soon, he gets near enough, nary a pace;
an identity now confirmed by a face.

5.7: In which Pedro provides a warning.

An identity now confirmed by a face.
Pedro runs off to inform his dear friend.
If the Captain suspects, finds any trace
that Isabelle's untrue, he'll meet his end.

"The Captain's back in town, or so you say?...
That development is quite worrisome...
But shouldn't he be with his wife... making hay?...
Why in the world to your Inn did he come?"

Pedro can do no more than speculate,
"Maybe Isabelle's admitted her lust...
She's forsaken him for you, told him straight...
And now your skull he is looking to bust!"

Though they try to hide from that fearsome ranger,
Columbine puts Oratio in danger.

5.8: IN WHICH A SERVANT NEEDLESSLY CAUSES TROUBLE.

Columbine puts Oratio in danger.
While the guy at the Inn (if you couldn't guess)
was not the Captain but just a stranger,
the real Captain's returned nevertheless.

Columbine spied him riding into the city
while still smarting from the beating she got.
She's sure the soldier will show no pity.
Tells the Captain a lie to stir the pot –

"Sir, welcome home, I'm afraid I must share...
In your absence, Isabelle's met a boy...
She's unfaithful, had a torrid affair!"
He is livid. The servant chuckles with joy.

While you wonder what's in Columbine's brain,
Oratio warns Isabelle to refrain.

5.9: In which an unwanted advance is rebuffed.

Oratio warns Isabelle to refrain.
Says this one-sided romance must conclude.
The Captain's both violent and insane.
"Safer if neither of us cross that dude."

She says, "What are you talking about?...
The Captain hasn't been seen for six years...
He couldn't hear us, even if we shout...
Come inside, lift my skirt, look at my rear."

"He's back, at the Inn, heard from a cleaner."
Isabelle is quite shocked to hear the news.
If he's returned, why hasn't he seen her?
Is he angry? Is he lost or confused?

While she runs to the Inn, starting to fret,
Columbine's gossip is not done quite yet.

5.10: In which a gossipy servant receives a just reward.

Columbine's gossip is not done quite yet.
Right up to Flamina's door she goes next.
"Wanted to tell you before I forget...
Just saw the Captain, seems awful vexed."

Flamina dumps her chamber pot on the maid.
But from her window she spies Isabelle
walking quickly, as if on a crusade.
Looks like she's headed straight for the hotel.

She thinks, "What if she professes her sin?...
And names Oratio as her paramour?...
That madman will pause his quest for his twin...
And kill my love in a fit of rancor!"

To save her boyfriend, she runs down the lane.
Flamina can't accept Oratio slain.

Flamina can't accept Oratio slain.
That means the Captain can't ever find out
that Isabelle resolved not to abstain,
and sought to grab Oratio's *lower snout.*

Oratio sees Flamina fly on by.
Assumes she is still mad at her rival.
But giving Isabelle another black eye
won't help ensure Oratio's survival.

He runs after her to prevent a fight.
Both of these maidens are known for thin skin.
Paused a second when he realized with a fright,
that Flamina just entered Pedro's Inn.

But back to that soon – we're not there just yet.
Isabelle comes with a plea and a threat.

5.12: In which Isabelle is reunited with a person she never met.

Isabelle comes with a plea and a threat
in the common room where he's drinking beers.
He looks at her as if they've never met.
She feels so betrayed, eyes welling with tears.

"My husband," she cries, "I've ached for your touch."
She slides her arms around his broad shoulders.
"Oh, joy! You've returned to me! As such...
Let's go home so I can grab your... boulders."

He politely moves her hand from his britches.
Hurt, she strikes back in desperation –
"Well then. I don't need you, nor your riches...
I have Oratio for fornication!"

As his character she starts to critique,
the real Captain arrives and starts to speak.

5.13: IN WHICH THE TWO BROTHERS ARE FINALLY REUNITED.

The real Captain arrives and starts to speak,
spies Isabelle talking to a strange bloke.
"I'm going to end that little pipsqueak!...
I'll chop off his head with one single stroke!"

"But wait," thinks the Captain, "...Could it be?...
My lost twin brother?... After all this time?...
And Isabelle! You've returned him to me!...
Must say, my love, you're a vision sublime!"

The Captain merrily hugs his family.
He forgets all 'bout Columbine's rumor.
Buys the patrons drinks, shakes hands (clammily),
and the three spend the night in good humor.

Others arrive as *two* Captains do speak,
uttering some ad-libbed lines, tongue-in-cheek.

5.14: In which everything ends happily.

"Uttering some ad-libbed lines, tongue-in-cheek?!?"
Flamina can't believe what she's seeing.
Everyone is happy. No reason to freak.
No concern 'bout Oratio's well-being.

"My Boy!" the Captain says to stunned Oratio.
"It's high time you married your fair lass."
Isabelle winks, "Captain, it's time to go."
Leaving, he pinches his lusty wife's round ass.

In the end, none were harmed, no one cheated.
Sorry if that wasn't what you expected.
Please don't blame the poet – it must be repeated:
Scala wrote this play; I just directed.

Curtain falls on this performance cliché.
They are just performers in a light play.

5: MASTERSONNET:

They are just performers in a light play.
A damsel, a Captain, and a twin brother.
A quick trip becomes a long time away.
Rivals for love resent one another.

Oratio faced an abundance of choice.
Pedro spies a mysterious stranger.
An identity that's confirmed by a voice.
Columbine puts Oratio in danger.

Oratio warns Isabelle to refrain.
Columbine's gossip is not done quite yet.
Flamina can't accept Oratio slain.
Isabelle comes with a plea and a threat.

The real Captain arrives and starts to speak,
uttering some ad-libbed lines, tongue in cheek.

ORATIO

Crown No. 6:

"Isabella's Fortune"

6.1: In which the setting of the story is described.

"Uttering some ad-libbed lines, tongue in cheek."
For this olden art form, that's tradition.
No one sticks to the script; they use technique
to give their lines comical addition.

Here's a typical tale of love and disguise,
a bit ribald (by medieval standard).
It's a light comedy, so no one dies
though many will be humbled and slandered.

Missing grooms, arranged marriages, cheating.
Normal happenings in Rome, 1610.
This play starts with two lovers meeting.
(It's Isabelle and the Captain again.)

But something said will leave her heart broken.
A promise is made, an oath is spoken.

6.2: IN WHICH A PROPOSAL IS MADE.

A promise is made, an oath is spoken
by the Captain, a man of high breeding.
Gave Isabelle a ring as a token
(which turned out to be a bit misleading).

"Isabelle, I admire your style...
Your porcelain skin and thick golden locks...
Please allow me to walk you down the aisle...
Then cook all my meals and darn all my socks."

Fair Isabelle considered his offer;
a man of fine breeding was quite a catch.
Good looks, fine clothes, and well... a full coffer,
so she and her dad agreed to the match.

But first, a quick trip to go meet a sheik.
Said he would only be gone for a week.

6.3: In which a fiancé of high breeding disappears.

Said he would only be gone for a week...
Business, in Naples, the Sheik conducted.
He and the Captain imported antiques.
The Bosporus Strait, the Turk had obstructed.

So they have to find another trade route
to get their fine goods to Rome's marketplace.
"Please don't be angry; don't cry and don't pout...
Just a week (or two) and then we'll embrace."

And so the Captain left with his vow,
but a week turned into almost three years.
No letters arrived – not even a "ciao."
She became the laughingstock of her peers.

For three years after being bespoken,
Isabelle lingered with her heart broken.

6.4: In which a maiden refuses a new proposal.

Isabelle lingered with her heart broken.
Her father, Pantaloon, tired of waiting,
says, "A new thought in me has awoken...
It's time, Isabelle, you resumed dating."

Pantaloon has a new suitor in mind.
Isabelle meets him but isn't in love.
While the guy is comely and not unkind,
it's the Captain she's convinced herself of.

Dressing up in the garb of a peasant,
she soon hops an oxcart and runs away.
Dreams that her reunion will be pleasant.
Didn't consider the Captain might stray.

But first, a subplot for which you'll be grateful:
Pedro's wife turned out not to be faithful.

6.5: In which a cuckold husband demand fealty.

Pedro's wife turned out not to be faithful.
(I assure you, these two plots will combine.)
His cheating wife, Columbine, was hateful
and stepping out with Dottore, that swine.

Unlike Pedro, Dottore was wealthy.
Gave Columbine that which Pedro could not.
Did not even bother to be stealthy.
Their constant canoodling left Pedro fraught.

If he told her twice, he told her ten times,
"Columbine, you are my wife, please desist...
No more Dottore, commit no more crimes!"
But his concerns, Columbine just dismissed.

Columbine called her husband 'Satan's spawn.'
The Captain, meanwhile, had simply moved on.

6.6: In which the Captain forgets his vow.

The Captain, meanwhile, had simply moved on.
Business resolved, he forgot Isabelle.
Travelled around, Verona and Milan.
One day, in love with Flamina he fell.

But she wanted nothing to do with that lout.
She loved Flavio, for whom she did pine.
Though a twist would put their future in doubt...
Flamina's dad was Dottore, the swine.

He would make a deal that would enrage her.
Dazzled by the Captain's large sack of gold,
Dottore decided to engage her
despite the fact the Captain's gross and old.

Flamina's friends are outraged by this bull.
Everyone calls his actions disgraceful.

6.7: In which the Captain fails to recognize someone important.

Everyone calls his actions disgraceful,
but the Captain's not bothered by chatter.
Until he has an encounter fateful
when a peasant overhears his patter.

As he stands under Flamina's window,
pitching his woo to the girl up above,
peasant Isabelle confronts her lost beau;
questions why he has forsaken her love?

He's confused, "I'd never love a peasant!"
Clearly, he has forgotten his old vow.
Shouts Flamina, "I find you unpleasant!...
I'm betrothed to Flavio, anyhow."

Stage Right, Flavio and his friend then come on.
Disrespect soon leads to swords being drawn.

6.8: In which Oratio falls in love during a battle.

Disrespect soon leads to swords being drawn.
The Captain can't see through Isabelle's disguise.
Flamina shouts down, "I hate you! Be gone!"
While the peasant catches Oratio's eyes.

Oratio's come to help Flavio's claim
to Flamina's hand (if push comes to shove).
But while the two suitors threaten to maim,
Oratio feels himself fall in love.

Though dressed in ragged clothes, covered in dirt,
he can clearly discern Isabelle's charm.
But first, his muscles he'll have to exert
to prevent Flavio coming to harm.

As the Captain's tossed into a pond,
the distressed damsels find reason to bond.

6.9: In which two maidens establish a friendship.

The distressed damsels find reason to bond
as, outmatched, the cowardly Captain flees.
Flamina talks to the peasant of blonde
while Flavio catches the Captain with ease.

"Can I help?" she asks, seeing Isabelle weep.
"He thinks I'm a peasant, not a Contessa."
Flamina tells her that jerk is a creep,
"You just need new clothes. Look through my dresser!"

She takes Isabelle in, brushes her hair,
draws her a bath, dresses her in a gown.
Soon Isabelle looks far more than just fair;
she's the most beautiful woman in town!

As they enjoy a girls' night after dark.
Dottore, the scoundrel, spies his next mark.

6.10: In which someone is being a creep.

Dottore, the scoundrel, spies his next mark
as the two beauties parade through the town.
"That girl, Isabelle, she gives me a spark...
Far more lovely than Columbine (that clown)."

"I must woo her to me, I must be swift...
Someone that fair won't be single for long...
But, first things first, I must buy her a gift...
And find a minstrel to sing her a song!"

He runs into the night to find flowers
as the two maidens drink ale and cavort.
They return to Flamina's in the wee hours
to relax with one last bottle of port.

All through the evening and morning beyond,
Oratio dreams of that beautiful blonde.

6.11: In which two rivals declare their intentions.

Oratio dreams of that beautiful blonde.
He can't get her sweet smile out of his head.
Of this 'peasant girl,' he is more than fond.
He resolves to wed her, sleep in her bed.

That morn' he runs to Flamina's at dawn,
poems in his heart, and candy in hand.
Over her beauty, he's prepared to fawn.
When he gets there, there's already a band?

Dottore is singing, making a scene.
Seems two suitors are asking her to choose.
Both yelling up, "I adore you, my queen."
"Isabelle, let me in. This guy? Excuse!"

Between these two, the difference is stark.
Just then, Columbine strolls in from the park.

6.12: In which a jilted lover arrives and makes trouble.

Just then, Columbine strolls in from the park.
She wasn't looking for a fight that morn',
but she overhears Dottore's remark
that he loves Isabelle because she's 'high-born.'

"How dare you say I'm not enough for you!"
(Columbine's low-born so his words really hurt.)
Kicks him in the shin, hits him with her shoe.
"Nevermore will you get under my skirt!"

Meanwhile, Isabelle looks down from above.
Oratio is just staring up, drooling.
He's enamored, shaking, clutching foxglove.
Just then, Flavio returns from dueling.

When you thought this tale can't go more astray,
Pedro won't stand to be a divorcee.

6.13: In which an unwanted suitor is chased away.

Pedro won't stand to be a divorcee.
He walks by and sees the man screwing his wife.
"Dottore, you swine! I've come here today...
To beat you within an inch of your life!"

With that, Dottore runs off in disgrace.
Followed by Pedro and Columbine, too.
Flavio asks his love to leave this place.
"Let's go to the church *now* to say 'I do.'"

Dottore is not around to protest.
The Captain's gone, too, tossed into the lake.
Off they go. Flamina's not even dressed.
The band sets off to find a wedding cake.

One loose end is left 'fore we end this play.
Some jokes are tame, some bawdy and risqué.

6.14: IN WHICH ISABELLE FINALLY FINDS TRUE LOVE.

Some jokes are tame, some bawdy and risqué.
Some loves takes time, some happen in seconds.
His love at first sight is on full display.
"Oratio, join me upstairs," she beckons.

He bounds upstairs where she waits in her peignoir.
"I'm impressed you loved me as a peasant...
Don't care if my dad's a fool or a tsar....
You love me for me. Find that... quite pleasant."

And so, for the first time, two lovers kiss.
And kiss and kiss more (you know how it goes).
Let's end here; we do not need to see this,
but as we exit... He's nibbling her toes.

They don't leave her boudoir for a whole week,
uttering their ad-libbed lines, tongue in cheek.

6: MASTERSONNET:

Uttering some ad-libbed lines, tongue in cheek.
A promise is made, an oath is spoken.
Said he would only be gone for a week.
Isabelle waited, with her heart broken.

Pedro's wife turned not to be faithful.
The Captain, meanwhile, had simply moved on.
Many would call his actions disgraceful.
Disrespect would soon lead to swords drawn.

The distressed damsels find reason to bond.
Dottore the scoundrel spies his next mark.
Oratio dreams of Isabelle's hair of blonde.
Just then Columbine strolls into the park.

Pedro won't stand to be a divorcee.
Some jokes are tame, some bawdy and risqué.

PULCINELLA

Crown No. 7:

"Intermezzo"

7.1: In which an intermission begins.

Some jokes are tame, some bawdy and risqué.
Sometimes an actor must just improvise.
To perform a *lazzo*, they stop the play
and do something bizarre as a surprise.

In Commedia, 'twas part of the show.
(Something of an intermission of sorts.)
Often, they called it an *intermezzo*.
Physical humor, and juggling, and sports!

We've now reached about halfway through this book
so it seems as good a time as any
to give some minor characters a look,
be they *Vecchi*, *Innamorati*, or *Zanni*.

Sandroné starts with a prank that's benign –
After work, Pantaloon craves some fine wine.

7.2: In which the Lazzo of the Straw is performed.

After work, Pantaloon craves some fine wine.
A pleasant draught to ease his wearied head.
He fills his cup with a vintage, divine,
while a velvet settee acts as his bed.

His servant, Sandroné, hides behind his back,
and with a long straw sneaks a subtle sip.
Each time Pantaloon reaches for a snack,
the cup is emptied with another dip.

Somehow, poor Pantaloon cannot detect
this trick that robs him of his sweet delight.
He pours and pours, but his thirst goes unchecked
and Sandroné mocks him, hidden from sight.

The wine close to his lips, yet so far away;
more tempting than a sumptuous buffet.

7.3: In which the Lazzo of the Fire is performed.

More tempting than a sumptuous buffet,
the feast was set. A banquet fine and grand.
Tartaglia prepared to dine away;
his guests' stomachs were ready to expand.

But through the door, with panic in his eyes,
Comes Gianduja, breathless, full of dread.
"The kitchen's ablaze! Flames are on the rise!"
So Tartaglia and the guests all fled.

Gianduja seems not troubled the least.
Sits down at the table, beaming with pride.
With fork in hand, claims the bountiful feast.
T'was never a fire. The servant had lied.

Tonight, he's the one who'll get to dine
while wearing a hat of chic, new design.

7.4: In which the Lazzo of the Floating Hat is performed.

While wearing a hat of chic new design,
La Signora walks with panache, head held high.
But then her hat floats up off her hairline.
Above her pate it flutters, swift and sly.

As she reaches up, it begins to sway.
An odd dance ensues, and try as she might,
her fingers grasping, it does drift away.
It dodges left, then spirals into flight.

As the chase unfolds, her dress too takes wing.
It lifts and twirls like leaves in a breeze.
The fabric flies up (that naughty plaything),
exposing the bloomers 'neath her chemise.

Let's leave La Signora 'fore she grows nuder.
Does the Captain detect an intruder?

7.5: In which the Lazzo of the Mirror is performed.

Does the Captain detect an intruder?
Is there a shadow stirring in the night?
His heart beats with fear, his hands are unsure.
He rises, draws his sword to face the fright.

"Who's there?" he whispers. His voice sounds shaken.
The mute intruder continues to lurk.
"Why, from my slumber, did you awaken?...
Be you a Moor? Or a thief?! Or a Turk?!?"

He moves through his bedroom, lights a candle.
He finds not a foe, but just his own gaze.
A mirror mocks him, a cowardly scandal,
reflecting his fear and face all ablaze.

While the Captain faces dangers picayune,
Scapino's mistress will be home quite soon.

7.6: In which the Lazzo of the Fly is performed.

Scapino's mistress will be home quite soon.
Ruffiana's tired, wants to go to sleep.
"I'll take no visitors this afternoon."
"Not a fly is in there," the servant peeps.

Ruffiana enters her palazzo
to find it filled to the rafters with guests!
The Doge, baronets, and a paparazzo,
trapeze artists, clowns, elephants, and pests.

The mistress runs outside, mad at the youth.
"Scapino, you lied! Why should you not die?"
"My lady, I'm innocent, I told the truth...
Inside your house is not a single *fly!*"

Next door from where the Lady's guests pursued her,
a maiden learns music from her tutor.

7.7: In which the Lazzo of the Stopped Music is performed.

A maiden learns music from her tutor.
Rosine yearns to learn kissing, not to sing.
Lindor the teacher longs to... instruct her.
Her supple body, his eyes worshipping.

But her dad Dottore (a chaperone)
watches and listens and she sings her song.
He falls asleep! Finally, they are alone,
but their make-out session doesn't last long.

When they kiss, Rosine stops singing, grows mute.
The silence rouses Dottore awake.
She quickly resumes her musical pursuit.
Dottore drifts off again with a shake.

As this keeps happening from morning 'til noon,
a chef's in the kitchen, with a large spoon.

7.8: In which the Lazzo of the Food is performed.

A chef's in the kitchen, with a large spoon.
Mezzetino stirs the pot, singing a rhyme.
He tosses in shoes, a broom, and a prune.
"Why not?" he says, "Let the flavors combine?"

A book of poems, socks, parsley, toy horse.
A spoonful of buttons, hankie of lace.
Each ingredient... a curious choice.
He stirs and stirs with a grin on his face.

A skunk, a hat, some broken porcelain,
A ribbon of velvet, some glass beads too.
He seasons the soup with a mandolin,
and tastes it, "Ah! 'Tis perfect! Just for you!"

After dinner while guests complain and rant,
Coviello's on-stage to brag of his aunt.

7.9: In which the Lazzo of the School of Humanity is performed.

Coviello's on-stage to brag of his aunt.
"A woman of wisdom, grace, and of might!"
Her 'School of Humanity' seeks a grant
so all can learn kindness, compassion, and right.

With passion, he speaks of her noble cause,
how she lifts the fallen and guides the lost.
Her lessons are pure, without any flaws.
"A beacon to all who would pay the cost."

But behind the curtain, the truth unfolds.
His aunt runs a... different... kind of trade.
That sinful teacher sells her body for gold!
(Through innuendo her vocation is laid.)

And since, for her favors, many compete,
two stubborn men for the first time will meet.

7.10: In which the Lazzo of the Handshake is performed.

Two stubborn men for the first time will meet
and with firm handshake stretch the bounds of grace.
Their palms intertwine as they do compete.
Each rival refusing to cede his place.

Arlecchino laughs, twists his arm all askance,
while Brighella grips hard and squeezes to maim.
Their bodies clash, a tug of strength and chance,
as each man struggles to victory claim.

As the men wrestle, words begin to fly.
They argue deep 'truths' of life and respect.
(Their illogic would make a philosopher sigh.)
Each one insisting his view is correct.

Let's leave, as the chance they'll give up is scant.
Pulcinella's allergic to a plant.

7.11: In which the Lazzo of the Sneeze is performed.

Pulcinella's allergic to a plant.
A daisy, perhaps? Or some springtime bloom?
He sniffs and sniffles but prevent it, he can't,
a sneeze so loud that it rattles the room.

After that sneeze comes a furious burst
and through this gale, some props knocked askew.
A teapot tumbled, silverware's dispersed,
the table flipped, and the dishes all flew.

Another sneeze! A louder, stronger force.
The backdrop quakes, the curtains rip in half.
A stagehand ducks, the actors knocked off course.
The set collapses as the audience laughs.

While this nose destroyed the playhouse, complete,
a growing organ is usually a treat.

7.12: In which the Lazzo of the Ever Growing Nose is performed.

A growing organ is usually a treat
but not when it's a nose that swells with lies.
Doctor Baloardo speaks bold and sweet,
though with each tale, his nose begins to rise.

He claims he fought with a lion through the night.
It's mane wild like fire... jaws ready to chew...
His nose extends as he describes the fight.
It betrays his claim the story is true.

With each fib he spins, his nose grows again.
Claims he is the Doge, owns a palazzo.
Baloardo's stories grow more insane.
(Pinocchio was based on this *lazzo*.)

We leave as the Doctor shouts he's a sheik.
Scaramouche's hair is luxurious and sleek.

7.13: IN WHICH THE LAZZO OF THE HAIRCUT IS PERFORMED.

Scaramouche's hair is luxurious and sleek.
His long, lavish locks are so fine and grand,
when Arlecchina, unskilled, but not meek,
decides to give him a trim, sword in hand.

With pure abandon, she swings her blade high.
The hair falls in clumps, uneven, not levelled.
With an errant slash, she cuts off his tie.
Soon, poor Scaramouche looks quite disheveled.

The shears come next, though their cuts imprecise.
With snip of cloth, a patch of skin's exposed!
Furious clippers continue to slice
'til soon Scaramouche's without any clothes!

All the players come out; they start to speak,
"Please let us practice our improv technique."

7.14: IN WHICH THE MINOR PLAYERS THANK YOU FOR THE OPPORTUNITY.

"Please let us practice our improv technique."
Sometimes *lazzi* are our sole chance to shine.
Some are good, though we admit most are weak
(mainly when we've gotten into the wine).

We need to give the main characters a break.
Those actors get tired or need to pee
and so us extras come on-stage to make
some mischief to amuse the bourgeoise.

But that's the end of this intermission.
Flavio's recovered from his fatigue.
You've all already paid your admission.
Let's return to plots of sex and intrigue!

So back to the rest of this matinee –
where some jokes are tame, some bawdy and risqué.

7: MASTERSONNET:

Some jokes are tame, some bawdy and risqué...
After work, Pantaloon craves some fine wine,
more tempting than a sumptuous buffet,
while wearing a hat of chic new design.

Does the Captain detect an intruder?
Scapino's mistress will be home quite soon.
A maiden learns music from a tutor.
A chef's in the kitchen with a large spoon.

Coviello's on-stage to brag of his aunt.
Two stubborn men for the first time will meet.
Pulcinella's allergic to a plant.
A growing organ is usually a treat.

Scaramouche's hair is luxurious and sleek,
"Please let us practice our improv technique!"

PEDROLINO

Crown No. 8:

"The Alexandrian Carpets"

8.1: In which a story about rugs is unrolled.

Please let us practice our improv technique;
otherwise, we cannot ever improve.
No bard gave us pre-written lines to speak.
We're making this up – please don't disapprove.

Renaissance Italy had many classes –
merchants, scoundrels, and commedia troupes
(with few decent folk mixed amongst asses.)
Here is a play 'bout all three of these groups.

'*The Alexandrian Carpets*' 'twas named.
But it's about so much more than just *rugs*.
Unfaithful lovers, someone wrongly blamed,
stolen merchandise, fools, gypsies, and thugs –

They all will appear. Some once and some twice.
In Bologna, cads lead a life of vice.

8.2: In which two rakish scoundrels are described.

In Bologna, cads lead a life of vice.
(Oratio and Flavio are the cads.)
Many once-chaste maidens did they entice
during years studying as undergrads.

Flavio took Flamina's maidenhood.
His friend Oratio took Isabelle's, too.
These two cavaliers were up to no good;
made marriage proposals they soon withdrew.

After their conquests, school ends, they go home.
Two deflowered maidens made a mistake.
The two boys head back to their fathers in Rome.
Two deflowered maidens feel their hearts break.

These girls, though forsaken, were hardly meek.
Two scorned damsels left in a fit of pique.

8.3: In which two scorned maidens seek revenge.

Two scorned damsels left in a fit of pique.
Upset at the boys who stole their virtue.
To the city of Rome, they both would sneak.
Once there, violence would likely ensue.

But first, some disguises would be needed.
Isabelle dressed as a man – 'Fabrito.'
That would allow her to pass unimpeded
(since women can't travel incognito).

Flamina takes on the guise of a soothsayer –
crystal ball, black hat, long, flowy dress.
With that, she could approach her betrayer,
tell his fortune, trick him, make him confess.

Meanwhile, a father seeks some advice.
An accusation's made that's not very nice.

8.4: IN WHICH A MERCHANT FINDS HIS PROPERTY MISSING.

An accusation's made that's not very nice.
Pantaloon bellows at his son's servant,
"You've led Oratio to a life of vice...
Don't say you haven't; I'm quite observant!"

"My Lord," says Pedro, "I'm just his attendant...
I have no control over that bad seed...
Know how you're missing your carpets, splendent?...
Oratio stole them... to buy some more meade!"

Pedro is lying to save his career.
He stole those carpets, with intent to sell.
They are stashed in a warehouse near here,
until he meets the black market cartel.

Hoping that his purse soon will be swollen,
Pedro looks to sell goods that are stolen.

8.5: In which a disreputable transaction is proposed.

Pedro looks to sell goods that are stolen.
In a tavern, he awaits his contact.
He's already late to meet friends for bowling.
The Fence arrives at three-thirty, exact.

"Next to Trevi Fountain, there is a warehouse...
Meet me there, two days' time. Bring lots of gold."
Flamina, nearby, overhears the louse.
Maybe these scoundrels need their fortunes told...

She comes over to them, rubbing her ball.
Her eyes rolling back; her chest starts to heave.
"I see everything, no matter how big or how small...
And the spirits tell me... you are both *thieves!*"

As she laughs at the thugs running in fear,
Flavio learns of an all-seeing seer.

8.6: In which a scoundrel receives an ominous warning.

Flavio learns of an all-seeing seer
as he's at the market buying more wine.
Pedro runs into him, acting all queer,
"Met a gypsy who sent shivers down my spine...

"She knew all my secrets, without question...
Flavio! Avoid that fortune-teller...
Else you'll need a priest to make a confession...
She'll see all your sins. Her third eye is stellar!"

As Pedro absconds, Flavio wonders –
Was it a mistake to leave Isabelle?
Was coming to Rome an awful blunder?
If he asked nicely, would the mystic tell?

Did she hate him? Her virginity stolen.
He seeks advice, eyes teary and swollen.

8.7: In which a repentant scoundrel seeks advice from the stars.

He seeks advice, eyes teary and swollen,
from someone he doesn't realize he knows.
Flamina's disguise has fooled the Roman.
He can't see beyond her clairvoyant's clothes.

With fifty florins, he crosses her palms.
"Does Isabelle love me, though I took flight?...
I shouldn't have left her. I'm full of qualms...
Tell me, seer – is there time to make it right?"

Flamina's shocked. Seems as if he's sincere.
The devilish rascal had a change of heart.
Reading his palm, "Good Sir, you've naught to fear...
Return to your love and ne'er shall you part."

While that's all going on... somewhere else near,
Oratio finds a sympathetic ear.

8.8: In which a repentant scoundrel seeks advice from a complete stranger.

Oratio find a sympathetic ear
while at the tavern drowning his sorrows.
A tourist sits next to him with a beer
while he's dreaming of his lost tomorrows.

He talks of his problems to 'Fabrito.'
"I loved a girl in Bologna, but fled."
(That 'tourist' is Isabelle incognito...)
"A hasty decision that I now dread."

"Tell me more about this maiden," says the tourist.
"I treated her bad. Flamina was her name...
Her figure soft, her heart the purest...
I sullied her honor; I'm filled with shame."

While Oratio pines for Flamina's hugs,
Pantaloon searches for the thieving thugs.

8.9: In which a merchant seeks to recover his lost goods.

Pantaloon searches for the thieving thugs.
His offspring's pilfering has made him sick.
His son's head likely 'tween a harlot's dugs.
Intends to beat him with this here big stick.

Crosses paths with Oratio conversing.
That little guy must be the rugs' buyer!
"This illicit sale, I'll be reversing...
And you, wicked rogue – I'll set you on fire!"

He grabs Oratio's neck, begins to squeeze.
That Pantaloon's a nasty curmudgeon.
So 'Fabrito' nimbly dodges and flees
lest 'he' get hit with the old man's bludgeon.

As 'he' looks for a secure location,
two scorned damsels share key information.

8.10: In which two maidens unexpectedly reunite.

Two scorned damsels share key information
as Isabelle searches for a place to hide.
Recognized, though disguised (to their elation),
when 'Fabrito' and the mystic collide.

Outside a warehouse near Trevi Fount;
reunited, after all they've been through.
Of their travels, they first give an account.
"I have something to say!" "You first!" "No, you!"

"Flavio loves you; he's full of regret."
"Oratio loves you, claims he made a mistake."
Both – "We came here to kill those rakes, and yet..."
"I have a plan! Meet me here at daybreak!

Gives her directions, "Don't worry 'bout the bugs."
Isabelle hides under some purloined rugs.

8.11: In which Flamina enacts a complex plan.

Isabelle hides under some purloined rugs
after following Flamina's direction.
Switches her boy clothes for ones a bit more snug
and awaits her Oratio's affection.

Flamina, meanwhile, finds Oratio,
as the old man drags his son down the street.
"Pantaloon," the mystic cries, "You must know...
At dawn, in Trevi, the true thieves will meet!"

Task one now done, she finds Flavio next.
Reads his palm, says she can sense his heartbreak.
He's under a spell. To relieve the effects,
he must arrive at Trevi by daybreak.

Flamina's plan deserves an ovation.
Oratio still dreams of fornication.

8.12: In which the players converge upon a storehouse.

Oratio still dreams of fornication,
nodding off in the alley, next to his dad.
While Pantaloon only dreams of castration;
he's going to hurt that rug-buyer bad.

They watch as, at dawn, a slim figure creeps.
Enters the warehouse where the carpets lie.
From behind some oak barrels, Pantaloon leaps,
"Wake up, son," he says, "Let's go get that guy!"

Flavio arrives a moment behind.
Came at the seer's guidance to end his curse.
The three go inside, but all that they find –
Some stolen carpets, boy clothes, and a purse.

Although the men look around for that goon,
the burglar is not found by Pantaloon.

8.13: In which a successful disguise is lowered.

The burglar is not found by Pantaloon.
"I saw him enter; he will not evade!"
The seer steps out, "By the light of the moon...
No one is here 'cept a beautiful maid."

As if on cue, Isabelle is revealed.
"Old Man, the thief you seek is your servant...
Pedro stole these carpets, had them concealed...
You'd have known this if you were observant."

Oratio can't believe Isabelle's here.
Pantaloon can't believe Pedro's so disloyal.
"That vile servant of mine – I'll make him pay dear...
I'll whip him harshly, then boil him in oil!"

While Pantaloon thinks himself a wily tycoon,
the *Vecchio* is an old, rich buffoon.

8.14: In which a everyone gets exactly what they
deserve.

A *Vecchio* is an old, rich buffoon.
An *Innamorato* is a young, love-struck fool.
The merchant runs off to find his spontoon
while poor Oratio does nothing but drool.

Flavio is the last problem to cure.
Flamina pulls off her mystic's disguise.
Gives her suitor a look that less than pure.
Both scorned damsels have now obtained their prize.

Nothing is left to do but quickly wed.
"No time to plan; let's just elope," they thought.
"We don't need bouquets or dresses," they said,
"And we can make up our vows on the spot."

Off the couples go, a priest they do seek
so as to practice their improv technique.

8: MASTERSONNET:

Please let us practice our improv technique!
In Bologna, cads lead a life of vice.
Two scorned damsels left in a fit of pique.
An accusation's made that's not very nice.

Pedro looks to sell goods that are stolen.
Flavio learns of an all-seeing seer.
He seeks advice, eyes teary and swollen.
Oratio finds a sympathetic ear.

Pantaloon searches for the thieving thugs.
Two scorned damsels share key information.
Isabelle hides under some purloined rugs.
Oratio still dreams of fornication.

The burglar is not found by Pantaloon.
A *Vecchio* is an old rich buffoon.

BURRATINO

Crown No. 9:

"The Two Faithful Notaries"

9.1: IN WHICH A PLAY ABOUT LOVERS AND LAWYERS IS LAID OUT TO THE AUDIENCE.

A *Vecchio* is an old, rich buffoon.
(That's Pantaloon and Gratiano here.)
Their hypocrisy is often lampooned
when scheming servants (the *Zanni*) appear.

But Commedia also needs lovers.
This silly play has not one, but two pairs.
Each kept apart by a father who hovers.
They need a trick to conceal their affairs.

'*Two Faithful Notaries*' to the rescue
(or at least people pretending as such)
who'll set this complicated plot askew.
(Sorry the melodrama's a bit much).

Although pre-marital sex is a disgrace,
a maiden's cold bed is a lonely place.

9.2: In which two maidens seek amorous company.

A maiden's cold bed is a lonely place.
Isabelle pines for Oratio's... vigor.
She's virtuous, pious, far too long chaste,
and really needs him to... squeeze her trigger.

"Columbine," she calls to her loyal servant,
"Find that man, sneak him into my bedroom...
My dad, Gratiano's, not too observant...
Still, send Oratio 'round in costume."

Next door, lives the daughter of a miser.
Flamina hopes Flavio will sneak in
leaving her dad, Pantaloon, none the wiser.
Anticipation makes her knees weaken.

As the sun sets, by the light of the moon,
from a dark alley, a lover doth croon...

9.3: In which two lusty maidens make tragic errors.

From a dark alley, a lover doth croon.
The dulcet tones draw Isabelle's attention.
Though hard to see by the light of the moon...
...Must be Oratio seeking affection.

She tosses her key down to the dark stranger.
But that's not her boyfriend in the shadow!
She doesn't realize that she's now in danger;
Spaventa lets himself in down below.

Next door, Flamina, too, flirts by mistake
when Gratiano wanders past, half-drunk.
She invites Isabelle's dad to... partake
(though she meant to lure Flavio to her bunk).

Of course, neither knave will get past first base –
Out of a window comes flying a vase!

9.4: In which a scoundrel is ejected.

Out of a window comes flying a vase!
Soon followed by a bowl of polenta.
"My virtue, how dare you try to debase...
Get the hell out of my house, Spaventa!"

"But... but..." stammers Spaventa dodging flak.
Trips over his cloak and rolls down the stairs
as Pantaloon and Pedro are coming back
from a long day handling business affairs.

"Stop being a pest." They pull out their sticks
and proceed to give Spaventa some blows.
The knave runs off dodging Isabelle's kicks.
Pantaloon heads home to change into bedclothes.

Surprised to learn Flamina's not asleep...
Shouts are heard, "Gratiano! You're a creep!"

9.5: IN WHICH A MISTAKE RESULTS IN AN UNWANTED
   BETROTHAL.

Shouts are heard, "Gratiano! You're a creep!"
followed by the old man bounding out the door.
He falls to his knees and begins to weep,
"Pantaloon! Don't beat me, I beg and implore."

"Your daughter was the one who invited me...
Said she loved me and wanted some kissing...
I accepted her call, ran up there with glee...
Then things got weird. Don't know what I'm missing?!?"

"Grati, my neighbor," says Pantaloon, "Please...
You've put my Flamina's honor in doubt...
Now you must wed her to set me at ease...
You've been in her bed; you cannot back out."

While Gratiano prepares to be wed,
the next morning, Isabelle stays in bed.

9.6: In which Isabelle becomes lovesick.

The next morning, Isabelle stays in bed
as the two old men plan in the courtyard.
So many wedding guests will need to be fed.
Must first hire caterers, priests, and a bard.

They are interrupted by Columbine,
"Gratiano! Your daughter is a mess...
My mistress just lies in bed, supine...
Refuses to eat, take a bath, or get dressed."

The two old men ponder as to the cause.
"Could it be she's fallen under a hex?"
"Bet that rogue Spaventa did this because...
He's upset that Isabelle refused him sex."

Course, that's not why Isabelle's losing sleep;
while to Harlequin, Flamina does weep.

9.7: In which Flamina laments her situation.

While to Harlequin, Flamina does weep,
"This can't be happening, must be a jest...
Tell me, dear valet, that I'm still asleep...
How could father betroth me to that pest?!?"

"He's short, he's bald, his palazzo is small...
His farts have the vague scent of oregano...
Much too weak to give me a fancy ball...
How will I explain this to Flavio!?!"

Harlequin sees she's quite melancholy.
He wants to help, but this is quite a big mess.
Lacking brains to concoct more than folly,
he must find accomplices to seek redress.

The servants meet, put together their heads.
"We three need a plan," the servants all said.

9.8: In which three foolish servants plan two clever pranks.

"We three need a plan," the servants all said.
Murder, of course, is the first thing that they think.
...And the second.... But the third time, instead,
"How 'bout a prank?" Pedro says with a wink.

He's the smartest fool in this coterie.
"First, we must obtain some black robes that flow...
So our guy can pass as a *notary*."
(A medieval lawyer, if you didn't know.)

It's Harlequin's task to get fancy clothes.
Pedro, meanwhile, will spread superstition.
Columbine will use her sensitive nose.
The three leave to get into position.

Their mistresses will wake to a surprise.
All it will take is a few clever lies.

9.9: In which Pedro tells a fib.

All it will take is a few clever lies
(and Flavio and Oratio with masks).
Pedro searches Venice until he spies
Spaventa sleeping beneath some wine casks.

"Spaventa, you drunk," Pedro shakes him awake.
"Isabelle's *pretending* to have gone mad...
If you *cure* her, her hand she'll let you take...
Just have to trick Gratiano, her dad."

The trap now laid, Pedro does not linger.
Tells two dads that Spaventa's a physician
"who can cure madness by waving his finger!"
Two gullible men have no suspicion.

Although Spaventa thinks he'll soon marry,
rumors begin to spread all 'round the sestiere.

9.10: IN WHICH A RUMOR ABOUNDS REGARDING A CURIOUS SCENT.

Rumors begin to spread all 'round the sestiere,
that Gratiano... well... that he smells foul.
While the details of the smell do vary,
it's oft' described as 'droppings of an owl.'

Columbine is the one sowing this tale;
she knows just how to make gossip spread quick.
Soon, in the taverns, over flagons of ale,
people question, "Is Gratiano sick?"

The rumor soon gets back to Pantaloon.
Wonders why he never noticed the stench.
"That guy does eat an awful lot of prunes...
Or worse yet... could Gratiano... be French!?!"

Pantaloon ponders what this all implies.
Flavio then arrives in his disguise.

9.11: In which an unexpected notary offers his services.

Flavio then arrives in his disguise,
dressed in black robes, and putting on an act.
"A notary?" Pantaloon says with surprise.
"You called me to write a marriage contract."

"I guess I must have, but there's now some kinks."
"Are there?" Flavio says in a fake voice.
Pantaloon explains... it seems the groom *stinks.*
"Well then, we must discern Flamina's choice."

"Can't marry a lady without consent...
I must interview this unfortunate bride...
See if she's willing to accept the scent...
One sec..." the 'notary' then ducks inside.

While the bride speaks with the functionary,
Spaventa comes on stage being scary.

9.12: In which Spaventa imprudently performs a spell.

Spaventa comes on stage being scary.
His look gives Pantaloon apprehension.
Isabelle comes down, seeming unwary
(she's in on the prank, I forgot to mention).

Gratiano arrives, "Please cure my girl!"
Spaventa, in turn, casts a spell, pretend.
Waves his hands and gives his fingers a whirl
and, just like that, Isabelle's madness ends.

"I'm cured, father!" she said and then smiled.
She runs back upstairs to get herself dressed.
Plain for all to see, Isabelle's beguiled.
Spaventa assumes everyone's impressed.

But he'll find himself out on his fanny...
Pedro makes an accusation, canny.

9.13: In which Pedro springs his trap.

Pedro makes an accusation, canny...
"He's not a real doctor; that was witchcraft...
A warlock once did that to my granny...
And soon after, she fell down a mine shaft!"

"This seems like a serious accusation,"
says a stranger whom everyone missed.
"There must be a long investigation...
I'm a notary – I'm here to assist."

Oratio (in costume) then does suggest,
"I must interview this unfortunate bride...
To see if she's cured or simply possessed...
One sec," the 'notary' then ducks inside.

It happens before the dads ask, "Wait, can he?"
Devious servants comprise the *Zanni*.

9.14: In which two marriages are consummated.

Devious servants comprise the *Zanni*.
Devious suitors get what they came for.
As they explore every... nook and cranny,
they deflower the maids – three times or more.

Finally, the damsels satisfied their urge.
Then, dressed in no more but a soiled sheet,
they throw open the windows and emerge.
"Father!" they call, "Our fiancés, please meet!"

It's far too late now. The deed has been done.
No choice but to accept these sons-in-law.
Two couples' marriages have just begun.
Three servants again outwit the bourgeois.

Curtain falls as Spaventa starts to swoon.
That *Vecchio* is an old, rich buffoon.

9: MASTERSONNET:

A *Vecchio* is an old, rich buffoon.
A maiden's cold bed is a lonely place.
From a dark alley, a lover doth croon.
Out of a window comes flying a vase.

Shouts are heard, "Gratiano, you're a creep!"
The next morning Isabelle stays in bed.
While to Harlequin, Flamina does weep.
"We three need a plan" the servants all said.

"All it will take is a few clever lies...."
Rumors begin to spread all 'round the sestiere.
Flavio then arrives, in a disguise.
Spaventa comes on stage, being scary.

Pedro makes an accusation canny.
Devious servants comprise the *Zanni*.

ARLECCHINA

Crown No. 10:

"He Who Was Believed Dead"

10.1: In which the Italian Renaissance is hastily described.

Devious servants comprise the *Zanni*,
but the term includes milkmaids and peasants.
Back then, for those born a serf or a nanny,
life was likely hard, short, and unpleasant.

Not to mention, wars dotted the region.
Men like the Captain sought glory and wealth.
Leaving widows behind every season
who'd have to seduce new husbands by stealth.

Oratio just wanted to be a merc.
He's why this play's named, '*He Who Was Believed Dead.*'
Isabelle, the widow, acted the jerk,
trying to lure the chaste lad to her bed.

But before we get that love story rollin'...
Pantaloon finds his gold has been stolen.

10.2: IN WHICH A MISER LOSES A PORTION OF HIS WEALTH.

Pantaloon finds his gold has been stolen.
In 1610, Florence, there were no banks.
Stored your wealth in your safe or your colon,
whether in scudi or florins or francs.

Pantaloon's coffers often overflowed
despite the fact his son was a deadbeat.
Without watchful eye, Flavio 'borrowed'
gold to spend keeping his harlots discrete.

Course that was just a few coins here and there
(to be expected with a wastrel son),
but this eve', the entire coffer was bare.
Not a florin was left – not even one!

While the miser searches each nook and cranny,
the widow won't sit back on her fanny.

10.3: In which a lusty widow schemes for romance.

The widow won't sit back on her fanny.
From her window, she watched Oratio train.
His locks of gold... his muscles uncanny...
So filled with passion, she went half-insane.

Oratio dreams of the Italian War,
fighting the Turk or the Spanish Armada.
Perhaps the Captain could be his mentor?
He'd spent all his coin on a fine spada.

Isabelle calls down, "I know the Captain well...
Come inside, I'll make an introduction."
Oratio rushes over, rings her doorbell.
Meanwhile, Isabelle plans her seduction.

A noble lad's virtue's 'bout to be stolen;
Isabelle lurks with lips moist and swollen.

10.4: In which a virtuous lad rebuffs a lascivious offer.

Isabelle lurks with lips moist and swollen
while Oratio waits tensely on her chaise longue.
Plays him a love song on her vi-olin.
Then she jumps on his lap, slips him her tongue!

She pins him down. She'll get what she's after.
"Oratio," she moans, "You're hung like a bull!"
His pleas for mercy just met by laughter
as she reaches down and grabs a handful.

The chaste boy seeks not passion, but battle.
Pushes her away. Her offer declined.
Offended that she treated him like chattel.
Flees the widow's home, leaves his sword behind.

He runs off. Isabelle feels dejected.
Lies cool the sting of being rejected.

10.5: In which a spurned widow does something petty.

Lies cool the sting of being rejected.
Pantaloon's outside, looking under a rock.
None of his florins have been collected.
A plan for revenge, she does concoct.

"Neighbor," he calls out, "Did you see the thief?"
Isabelle responds, "Oh, I know that whelp...
I did spy the crook, and let me be brief...
Oratio stole your coins... with Pedro's help."

"My servant Pedro stole gold from my chest?!?...
Seems he's not as loyal as he portrayed...
I'll make a report; call for their arrest!"
Pantaloon runs off, feeling quite betrayed.

Not satisfied with that single result,
she informs the Captain of grave insult.

10.6: In which a fierce warrior's honor is insulted.

She informs the Captain of grave insult.
He is in the town square seeking recruits.
The few who are chosen often exult.
(They'll earn a uniform with shiny boots.)

"I hope Oratio will come and try out,"
the Captain mused as Isabelle walks by.
"Oratio?" she says, "He called you a lout...
Said he'd never fight for such a small fry."

A tear comes to the Captain's eye, "That's cruel...
I'll teach him who's a real condottiere....
Challenge that arrogant pup to a duel...
Won't be enough of him left to bury!"

Looks like Oratio might get dissected.
Pedro gathers all of those affected.

10.7: In which three wronged men plot revenge.

Pedro gathers all of those affected
when he hears there's a warrant for his arrest.
Upset that his master even suspected
that humble Pedro had emptied his chest.

Pedro provides proof to indict the real crook.
It was Flavio, Pantaloon's bad seed.
With that, Pantaloon lets him off the hook.
But how to avenge Isabelle's bad deed?

The pair talk to the Captain of her lies.
He's angry and wants revenge to be served.
Two villains, the men agree to chastise.
Pedro suggests a cruel prank well-deserved.

The first step done to achieve the result?
Flavio gets a proposition... adult.

10.8: In which Flavio received an unexpected offer.

Flavio gets a proposition, adult,
from Pedro, as he sits swilling some gin.
"I know two things. You and I must consult...
First, it's with Flamina you wish to sin."

"Heard from her servant she fancies you too...
Says she desires to make the two-backed beast...
But she's shy. Seeks a secret rendezvous...
And for that, a hidden room must be leased."

"But, I also heard you came into wealth...
If you pay me for my fair expenses...
I'll arrange to bring you to her by stealth...
Where you'll enjoy her with all of your senses."

That takes care of the thief; next is the liar...
"Oratio's in a position dire!"

10.9: IN WHICH PEDRO RETRIEVES A LOST SWORD.

"Oratio's in a position dire!"
is the tale he puts in Isabelle's ears.
"The Captain's looking to set him on fire...
The boy is in hiding, trembling with fears!"

Pedro tells the widow he's made a deal.
Oratio will trade sex for protection.
"If, from the Captain, you Oratio conceal...
You can have his love... without rejection."

Isabelle quickly agrees to the pact.
"Give me his sword as a sign of your word."
She does and provides directions, exact,
as well as coins for expenses incurred.

She waits until dusk, expecting to score.
Soon Pedro appears at Isabelle's door.

10.10: In which a rascal seeks carnal pleasures.

Soon Pedro appears at Isabelle's door,
with a figure dressed in a cloak and hood.
'Round the yard, the hidden key they look for.
It's where she left it – in a pile of wood.

The lamps are unlit, all is very dark
(in case the Captain is lurking nearby).
Took the long way through alleys and the park.
'Twas done to ensure Oratio won't die.

Once in the boudoir, Pedro softly states,
"Flavio, wait here, I'll bring in Flamina...
Speak not, just disrobe, and pray to the fates...
She's as randy as a wild hyena!"

She intends to ride him like a destrier.
The widow burns with white hot desire.

10.11: IN WHICH A WIDOW SLAKES HER THIRST.

The widow burns with white hot desire.
She slips into the room, starts to undress.
Last time she made love was five years prior.
Oratio's pizzle she seeks to caress.

She jumps the boy, throws him onto the bed.
Strange that his stomach feels a bit... thicker?
And there seems to be less hair on his head.
Instead of cologne... he smells of liquor.

But, no matter, Isabelle starts to think.
'Tis but a trifle, a trick of the night.
She slakes her lustful thirst, and deep she does drink
of manly Oratio's carnal delight.

Neither lover has an idea what's in store.
Hours making love on the bed and the floor.

10.12: In which the light of morning arrives.

Hours making love on the bed and the floor,
'til morning comes. The couple's passion spent.
Suddenly, at dawn there comes an uproar.
Seems the lovers made love without consent.

"You're not Oratio!," Isabelle exclaims,
"And you're not Flamina," shouts Flavio.
Both – "This is so gross – I feel so ashamed."
"I need a shower; you'd better just go."

Flavio is slow; he can't find his socks.
Dressing and leaving should not be this hard.
Isabelle can't stand to see this lummox
so she flees her house to wait in the yard.

This dumb play's moral will be revealed soon.
Those wronged have been righted under new moon.

10.13: In which a sudden betrothal is arranged.

Those wronged have been righted under new moon.
As Isabelle flees her house, steps outside,
the Captain is there, humming a tune,
"I dueled poor Oratio and he died."

"Thanks for alerting me of that knave's slight."
Her cruel lies have left Isabelle distraught.
If he's truly dead, she can't make this right.
But, one more lesson still needs to be taught...

Flavio comes down, runs smack into his dad.
"Son, this widow's honor you did besmirch...
Only one way for scandal not to be had...
You must marry her. Let's head to the church!"

Thus are made whole all those who have been hewn;
in this tale – the Captain and Pantaloon.

10.14: In which schemers learn a valuable lesson.

In this tale, the Captain and Pantaloon
get more than the two who got a spouse.
The Captain gets a man for his platoon
and Pantaloon gets a bum out of his house.

Oratio appears; his sword is returned.
He's off to join the Captain's campaign.
Pedro gives his master the florins he's earned.
The four conspirators toast with champagne.

Isabelle learned to not cross retainers.
Flavio learned to not steal from his sire.
The audience enjoyed entertainers
suffer consequence of being a liar.

Underlings are oft' 'scheme-y' and 'plan-y;'
Devious servants comprise the *Zanni.*

10: MASTERSONNET:

Devious servants comprise the *Zanni.*
Pantaloon finds his gold has been stolen.
The widow won't sit back on her fanny.
Isabelle lurks with lips moist and swollen.

Lies cool the sting of being rejected.
She informs the Captain of grave insult.
Pedro gathers all of those affected.
Flavio gets a proposition, *adult.*

Oratio's in a position dire.
Soon, Pedro appears at Isabelle's door.
The widow burns with white-hot desire.
Hours making love on the bed and the floor.

Those wronged will be righted under new moon;
In this tale – the Captain and Pantaloon.

COLUMBINA

Crown No. 11:

"The Dentist"

II.I: In which a toothless tale is introduced.

In this tale, the Captain and Pantaloon
are once more destined to fail getting wed.
By story's end, one will eat with a spoon;
the other is left a hanging plot thread.

'*The Dentist*' is a crook you shouldn't trust
('least 'fore they invented medical school).
True that Isabelle was filled with lust
but not for those jerks. She won't love a fool.

Oratio's father, Pantaloon schemed,
to get rid of his son (his love's rival).
But he'd end up getting more than he dreamed
after his servant, Pedro's, arrival.

While one won't ever again chew caramel,
all vie for the hand of the fair Isabelle.

II.2: In which a servant is brutally attacked by his master.

All vie for the hand of the fair Isabelle.
But let's start with Pantaloon's story first.
He talks of wooing the young demoiselle,
with his servant who with love is well-versed.

"Think I'll ask her to attend the soiree."
"But Master," Pedro cries, "She loves another."
"My wastrel son? Ha. I'll send him away...
Just the same as I did with his mother."

Pedro takes Oratio's side, "That's not fair...
Compared to you, the boy has much more charm."
Remarks that those two make a better pair.
Jealous Pantaloon then *bites* Pedro's arm!

Shocked that his master is acting the loon,
Pedro swears vengeance against the tycoon.

11.3: In which a grievously injured servant plans his revenge.

Pedro swears vengeance against the tycoon.
Teeth marks left in flesh are an awful slight.
Payback must be harsh, and stealthy, and soon.
But what's the proper response to a bite?

Then he overhears fair Isabelle moan.
She cries, "Oratio's being sent away!"
"Long distance?" "We've yet to invent the phone!"
"Flamina, what can we do to make him stay?"

Pedro interrupts, "We're on the same team."
He can help her, he suggests with some winks.
"But do me this favor, weird though it may seem...
Flamina, go tell Pantaloon he *stinks!*"

But just before he can describe the smell,
the servant crosses the Captain as well.

II.4: In which an unexpected suitor pitches woo.

The servant crosses the Captain as well,
when the soldier comes 'round to take his turn.
Steps up to the three, playing his vielle,
singing, "My dear, for you my heart doth burn."

The maidens are, let's say... less than impressed,
and both tell the would-be suitor to go.
But the rogue won't be deterred or repressed.
Pedro intervenes, "The ladies said 'no.'"

The Captain waves his battacio high,
"How dare you obstruct! You impudent clown!...
Next time I see you, you're likely to die!"
And with that, the Captain leaves with a frown.

Poor Pedro frets he's upset someone rich;
now it's Oratio's turn to make a pitch.

II.5: IN WHICH A STUDENT PROFESSES HIS LOVE.

Now it's Oratio's turn to make a pitch.
He catches up to Isabelle walking home.
"We are meant for each other; let's get hitched!...
I'll refuse to leave, stay with you in Rome."

Isabelle's pleased to hear his declaration.
She loves him too and soon his face is bussed.
But before they can complete their flirtation,
Pantaloon arrives... looking rather non-plussed.

"Oratio, ready yourself now to leave...
Your education in Perugia won't wait...
A carriage will take you tomorrow eve...
Go home and pack. There's no time for this date."

Thoughts of leaving make Oratio afraid.
Dottore is waiting to be repaid.

II.6: In which a gambling debt is settled.

Dottore is waiting to be repaid.
He soundly beat Pantaloon rolling dice.
But, though oft' promised, compensation's delayed.
He's still owed three hundred scudi, precise.

Pedro is aware of his master's debts,
and knows the bum's known as a freeloader.
Tells Dottore he'll retrieve his assets
if Dottore warns Pantaloon of 'an odor.'

"Just say his breath smells like a mule's arse...
And trust that will get you all you are owed."
Pedro's sincere, notes this is not a farce.
It's high time Pantaloon reaped what he sowed.

While Pedro hopes to make Pantaloon twitch,
conspiracies grow (to include a witch).

11.7: In which magic candy is introduced to the plot.

Conspiracies grow (to include a witch).
If only Pantaloon could be... dispatched.
Oratio's inheritance would make him rich,
with no one left to block getting attached.

Pasquale the witch will not murder for cash
though she'll give paranormal assistance.
She has just the concoction in her stash
to overcome Pantaloon's resistance.

"Here are two candies, one blue and one red...
The blue one will make a man go stark mad...
The other candy will clear his head...
A magic prank will melt the heart of that dad."

Two bags of candy bought. Ten scudi paid.
Two devious traps are 'bout to be laid.

11.8: In which a malodorous rumor spreads throughout Rome.

Two devious traps are 'bout to be laid.
First up is Flamina, Isabelle's friend.
She says to Pantaloon, "I'm quite dismayed...
She'll never love you while your breath offends."

Next up, Dottore, whom he sees on the street.
"Yikes, what is the stench coming from your face?!?...
Pantaloon, what in God's name did you eat?"
Embarrassed, the merchant flees in disgrace.

He later ponders what happened that day.
"I must accept they are telling the truth...
Can't be coincidence – must be decay...
It is clear that I've got a bad tooth."

And... the other plotline's a real dandy.
Yes, this story involves magic candy.

11.9: In which an erudite student loses his wits.

Yes, this story involves magic candy.
(Don't blame me, Scala penned it.)
Just consider it like some strong brandy...
Imbibe too much, you become a half-wit.

"Pedro," Isabelle asks, "Do be a dear...
Bring these to Oratio. Tell him to eat...
They aren't poisoned; this isn't King Lear...
Trust that with them, Pantaloon we'll defeat."

Pedro is happy to join in this prank.
He is still an angry, mischievous elf.
Soon Oratio is drooling, expression blank.
...Pedro pockets a candy for himself.

Pantaloon thinks his breath smells like manure.
An offer is made to provide a 'cure.'

II.10: In which an offending tooth is pulled.

An offer is made to provide a 'cure'
to relieve Pantaloon's mysterious stench.
He's approached by a masked dentist, obscure,
who proffers some brushes, a drill, and a wrench.

"The problem, Sir, is you have a bad tooth...
Let's pull it out and you'll smell like a rose...
Trust me, I'm a dentist known for the truth."
(It's Pedro in disguise, I should disclose.)

He goes to work on the old merchant's face.
Pulls several teeth on the left and the right.
Pedro leaves naught but sore gums and a space.
He unmasks, "That'll teach you to not bite!"

He capers off like a Spanish Grandee.
Pedro has angered the rich old dandy.

Pedro has angered the rich old dandy.
Pantaloon paid that fraud three hundred scudi!
The guy seemed legitimate and handy
but all he got was a mouth sore and bloody.

"I'll have my revenge!" He swears with a lisp.
He seethes with rage, shame, and a touch of sadness.
As he sips his gruel (can eat nothing crisp),
Flamina comes with a tale of madness.

"Pantaloon, come quick! Your son's gone insane...
Sending him away gave him such unease...
Maybe it was poison? Or something arcane?....
You need a doctor to cure his disease."

From reprisal, Pantaloon must detour.
Oratio suffers from madness, for sure.

11.12: In which Pantaloon seeks medical advice.

Oratio suffers from madness, for sure.
When Pantaloon arrives, he's just drooling.
The young man's regressed. He was once mature.
In this state, he can't finish his schooling!

Pasquale steps forth, Caduceus in hand.
"I'm a doctor. This man's condition is dire."
She examines the patient, feels his gland.
"To cure him, a bride must you acquire."

"Only *Isabelle* can scratch this boy's itch."
"But she's *my* beloved!" Pantaloon laments.
"There's no other option. Don't be a bitch."
Thus, to a marriage, Pantaloon consents.

Soon after they wed, they'll need a nanny.
No master can prevail 'gainst a *Zanni*.

11.13: In which Pantaloon mourns the loss of his servant.

No master can prevail 'gainst a *Zanni.*
Pantaloon soon remembers he's toothless.
When he finds Pedro, he'll kick his fanny!
Pulls out his stick, prepares to be ruthless.

Pedro comes to visit his Oratio.
But something's wrong. He's acting all foolish.
His brain's pudding. Lips have a strange blue glow.
To beat this imbecile... would be ghoulish.

"No way to cure him by finding a bride...
Such a shame, Pedro was once so clever...
For mercy, I'll put my vengeance aside."
Enough that he's dim-witted forever.

Once Pantaloon leaves to go gum mashed banan-y,
watch Pedro perform some trick uncanny.

II.14: In which two miraculous recoveries occur.

Watch Pedro perform some trick uncanny
now that his oppressor has gone off-stage.
It's high time to implement the plan he
and Isabelle had worked out to assuage.

Isabelle produces two candies, red.
One in each moron's mouth, Pasquale prescribed.
In minutes, the men both have a clear head.
The cure worked just as the witch had described.

Pedro takes his bow, leaves the stage to pay
Dottore his promised three hundred scudi.
Isabelle and Oratio hope this play
made some sense, with a plot not too muddy.

In Commedia, someone's always lampooned.
In this tale t'was the Captain and Pantaloon.

11: Mastersonnet:

In this tale, the Captain and Pantaloon
all vie for the hand of the fair Isabelle.
Pedro swears vengeance against the tycoon.
The servant crosses the Captain, as well.

Now it's Oratio's turn to make a pitch.
Dottore is waiting to be repaid.
Conspiracies grow (to include a witch).
Two devious traps are 'bout to be laid.

Yes, this story involves magic candy.
An offer is made to provide a "cure."
Pedro has angered the rich old dandy.
Oratio suffers from madness, for sure.

No master can prevail 'gainst a *Zanni*;
watch Pedro perform some trick uncanny.

IL DOTTORE GRATIANO

Crown No. 12:

"The Fake Magician"

12.1: In which two rival patriarchs are introduced.

Watch Pedro perform some trick uncanny
in a play entitled '*The Fake Magician.*'
Scala couldn't paint like Modigliani.
To be a playwright was his ambition.

So he wrote one about two merchant rivals
who each had raised two disobedient teens.
The four would not suffer love's deprivals.
Most lustful kids this side of the Apennines.

Pantaloon and Gratiano were neighbors
which made the four kids' rendezvouses easy.
Despite the two harried fathers' labors,
there were repeated encounters... sleazy.

While on four necks two couples were nibbling,
two rival merchants spend their days quibbling.

12.2: In which two sets of lovers are introduced.

Two rival merchants spend their days quibbling
over bushels of wheat and sacks of grain.
Busy counting coins and receipts scribbling,
dealing with spoiled children was such a pain.

Pantaloon's daughter was supposedly chaste,
but Flamina was tempted by a cur.
Oratio sought to her honor debase.
Gratiano's no-good son he must deter.

Of course, Gratiano had his own woes.
Flavio was Pantaloon's son and heir
who called to his daughter from the shadows,
tempting Isabelle into an affair.

Two girls who'd make their mothers a granny.
Two courtesans (with help from their *Zanni*).

12.3: IN WHICH ORATIO RISES TO THE OCCASION.

Two courtesans (with help from their *Zanni*).
Oratio is the first lover on stage.
"I need to bang her like a tympani...
Pedro, my servant, come and earn your wage."

Flamina awaits on the second floor.
Pedro appears with a ladder in hand.
Oratio's randy and looking to score.
As soon as night falls, all goes just as planned.

On Flamina's pleasures, he will soon dine.
Pantaloon already sleeps in his chair.
Up, up the suitor climbs with bottle of wine.
While below, her dad remains unaware.

From their lips, forbidden wine is soon dribbling.
Two lovers in love with each other's sibling.

12.4: IN WHICH FLAVIO LAYS DOWN SOME PIPE.

Two lovers in love with each other's sibling.
Flavio, the suitor, comes on stage next.
His passion for Isabelle is crippling.
"How to get into her room?" He is vexed.

Her servant Columbine has a good plan.
Tells Gratiano that there is a leak.
"Then hire a plumber!" squawks the tired old man.
Flavio, in disguise, arrives as they speak.

In fake moustache, he is led through the house.
The old merchant does not suspect a thing.
Though they have to be quiet as a mouse,
sly Flavio soon wears out her bedspring.

Four enjoy a night of concupiscence.
Passion, of course, has its consequences.

12.5: In which two unchaste maidens begin to expand.

Passion, of course, has its consequences
(especially when you neglect protection).
By that, I mean pregnancy commences,
which oft' leads to a father's rejection.

Flamina spends her mornings feeling ill.
Isabelle starts craving pickled ice cream.
(This was before they'd invented 'the pill'.)
Pantaloon and Gratiano would soon steam.

See, every day the damsels' bellies swell.
For now, Pantaloon thinks she's just fatter.
But soon he'll realize she's not just unwell.
"Obese... or pregnant?" Must be the latter!

Probably too late to make a confession
since wedding bells seem out of the question.

12.6: In which several methods to avoid scandal are contemplated.

Since wedding bells seem out of the question,
two young men must form an alternate plan.
Disgrace is looming from their indiscretion,
but neither of these two is a wise man.

"Our fathers hate one another with malice."
"No chance they would approve of a marriage."
"Put poison in their soup or wine chalice?"
"Cross our fingers and hope for miscarriage?"

They're out of ideas. They need Pedro's aid.
Wise and deceitful, he'll know what to do.
Pedro's happy to help (so long as he's paid).
This sort of prank is right in his purview.

He must break through two fathers' defenses.
Scandal brews, lest they come to their senses.

12.7: In which an ominous prediction is made.

Scandal brews, lest they come to their senses.
But how to bring stubborn mules to the table...?
Pedro calls Harlequin, pays his expenses,
and the two servants invent a fable.

Harlequin, dressed in soothsayer clothes,
confronts Pantaloon outside of his store.
"All things I see," he says, "All things I knows...
Flamina's not getting fat. There is more...!"

"My daughter?" Pantaloon's taken aback.
"Yes. Your child is sick, may die really soon...
She needs a doctor, and not just some quack...
I predict she'll be dead by the next moon."

Dad can't let her die of indigestion.
Perhaps the doctor has a suggestion?

12.8: In which a doctor is called upon.

Perhaps the doctor has a suggestion?
(The doctor is Columbine in disguise.)
"Could it be..." he asks, "lack of egestion?"
Columbine (not a doctor) tells him some lies –

"Pantaloon, I've examined your daughter...
I'm afraid that the prognosis is dire...
Can't cure her disease with holy water...
In order to live, she needs... a squire."

"That seems quite farfetched," Pantaloon muses.
"You question my skills?" Columbine responds,
"She must marry whomever she chooses...
The sole cure for her ills is wedding bonds."

"That's dumb," the audience criticizes.
In Commedia, there are always disguises.

12.9: In which several more disguises are donned.

In Commedia there are always disguises.
And like it or not, no one catches on.
Actors have costumes in all shapes and sizes.
We've four more to go before curtain's drawn.

Pedro brings out two sheets cut with eyeholes.
Flavio and Oratio will be ghosts.
They shamble around like poor unfortunate souls
and, after a briefing, head to their posts.

Harlequin dons his old soothsayer cloak.
In faerie garb, Columbine will be dressed.
Soon, the paranormal they will invoke.
And two stubborn dads will have some new guests...

To get sanction for four kids to marry –
a simple trick, but one that's quite scary.

12.10: In which two ghostly spirits walk the earth.

A simple trick, but one that's quite scary,
starts as two merchants return from their work.
Each casts a glare at their adversary.
Insults are thrown with a growl and a smirk.

Very immature for two patricians.
But a cold wind arises in the night,
and down the street float two apparitions!
The two bickering merchants cower with fright.

Pantaloon's speechless, quiet as a mouse.
Gratiano crouches down on the floor.
The first ghost floats into Pantaloon's house.
The second through Gratiano's front door.

Can the ghosts be banished 'fore the sun rises?
What's needed is a seer who advises.

12.11: IN WHICH A MAGICIAN CONVENIENTLY APPEARS.

What's needed is a seer who advises.
But where to find one at such a late hour?
"Pedro would know," Pantaloon surmises.
Pedro and friend arrive looking dour.

"Heard you were in need of a magician,"
says Pedro with a smile. "You can use *him*."
Harlequin – "Hire me… or a mortician…
Your daughters are in danger. It's looking grim."

The two fathers pay the soothsayer's wage.
He says his cant, twirls a magical staff.
Soon a faerie (Columbine) comes on stage,
sees two cowardly dads, starts to laugh.

The situation begins looking hairy.
Can they meet the demands of a faerie?

12.12: In which two patricians are given a solution.

Can they meet the demands of a faerie?
Columbine brings news from beyond the grave.
"The Powers need your daughters to marry...
Don't matter whether a prince or a knave."

"But they must be wed before the dawn breaks...
Or those ghosts will drag them into hell's cleft...
Trust me! I'm a faerie, for goodness sakes."
Saying no more, Columbine turned and left.

Gratiano, of course, seeks to comply.
Spirits, Pantaloon does not want to fight.
But at this hour, grooms are in short supply.
"How can we find two men before first light?"

But grooms, the dads won't need to discover.
A wizard is near to conjure a lover.

12.13: In which two suitable grooms are miraculously
    conjured.

A wizard is near to conjure a lover.
Harlequin the 'magician' saves the day.
"I'll summon both a man that will love her...
and I'll cast the spell for no extra pay!"

The soothsayer spins around and around;
he's chanting gibberish and flailing his limbs.
Soon, from the girls' bedrooms there comes a sound –
of shrieks, and moans, slamming bedframes, and hymns.

The two merchants haven't heard such a din
since their wives passed away some years ago.
It's the sound of passion, hunger, and sin.
When it dies down, Harlequin shouts, "Presto!"

Takes some time for the girls to recover.
Innamorati will meet undercover.

12.14: IN WHICH TWO FEUDING FAMILIES ARE COMBINED.

Innamorati will meet undercover,
exposed only when morning sun rises.
Flamina opens a window and above her
is that boy Pantaloon despises.

From Isabelle's window – Flavio's face...
and Isabelle looking quite satiated.
"Dad!" she cries, "Look who appeared in my space...
Seems like we're wed. I'm pregnant. We've mated."

"I'm pregnant, too!" Flamina tells her dad.
The two merchants shake hands. They're now in-laws.
They have no idea that they've just been had
by three wily servants, to the crowd's applause.

The audience loves when onstage comes a *Zanni*,
and Pedro performs some trick uncanny.

12: MASTERSONNET:

Watch Pedro perform some trick uncanny.
Two rival merchants spend their days quibbling.
Two courtesans (with help from the *Zanni*).
Two lovers in love which each other's sibling.

Passion, of course, has its consequences.
Though wedding bells seem out of the question.
Scandal brews, lest they come to their senses.
Perhaps the doctor has a suggestion?

In Commedia, there are always disguises.
A simple trick, but one that's quite scary.
What's needed is a seer who advises.
Can they meet the demands of a faerie?

A wizard is near to conjure a lover.
Innamorati will meet undercover.

SPAVENTA

Crown No. 13:

"The Lady That Was Believed Dead"

13.1: In which a commonly used plot device is described.

Innamorati will meet under cover.
That big word means 'sweethearts' in Italian.
Two courtesans – a man born to love her,
...and a girl that craves 'riding the stallion.'

'*The Lady Who Was Believed Dead*' 'tis named.
A tale 'bout poison and faking one's death
when family frustrates passion untamed,
forcing two lovers to take their last breath.

William Shakespeare's in Commedia's debt.
He used this plot in his famous play –
the one called 'Romeo and Juliet,'
(though that's a classic; this version's cliché).

Here in Verona – 1610 is the date –
it's not that often one finds a soulmate.

13.2: In which a horrible tragedy occurs.

It's not that often one finds a soulmate,
though Flamina found Oratio in school.
As teens, they met and soon started to date.
Later, he bought her a ring and a jewel.

Flamina's dad, Pantaloon, disagreed.
Oratio did not earn near enough cash.
She'd be betrothed to one of 'higher breed.'
When Flamina heard, she did something rash.

Faced with the loss of true love's wedded bliss,
she could not cope, drank poison, and died!
For Commedia, that's a shocking premise,
and none in Verona were left dry-eyed.

'Bove Flamina's tomb, angels now hover.
Will her forlorn suitor e'er recover?

13.3: In which Oratio keeps a scandalous secret.

"Will her forlorn suitor e'er recover?"
asks his friend Flavio, one day at lunch.
"Flamina's gone. There won't be another...
Want me to give that Pantaloon a punch?"

Oratio seems too depressed to respond.
He just sits silently stirring his soup
with furrowed brow under long locks of blonde.
(He's ashamed for making his friend a dupe.)

You see, Oratio knows something we don't.
That wasn't real poison; Flamina's not dead!
And as long as the pair's cover's not blown,
they'll soon reconnect, elope, and be wed.

At midnight, while in her tomb she'll await,
Oratio'll help Flamina avoid fate.

13.4: In which a romantic conspiracy is revealed.

Oratio'll help Flamina avoid fate.
After all, a dead girl can't be betrothed.
They'll wed while Pantaloon deals with probate
and, once that occurs, all can be exposed.

Flamina purchased a sleeping potion
and is lying peacefully in her crypt.
The funeral produced such emotion;
t'was hard for Oratio to stay tight-lipped.

Pedro, his servant, was the only man
who'd been told of the nefarious scheme.
That night, he'd sneak in, according to plan
and gently wake Flamina from her dream.

Meanwhile, her father is in disbelief.
Dottore helps comfort Pantaloon's grief.

13.5: IN WHICH A FATHER REGRETS HIS DECISION.

Dottore helps comfort Pantaloon's grief,
as they walk back home after the service.
"It's tragic my daughter's life was so brief...
Did her betrothal make her so nervous?"

"My friend, Oratio was quite a good catch...
I should know, he's my son," Dottore cried.
"Anyone else would cause Flamina to retch...
Forbidding their union is why she died."

Pantaloon knows; he is full of regrets.
But it's too late to cure what has occurred.
She was a good daughter, not some coquette,
and because of his greed, she's now interred.

While Pantaloon laments his choice of groom,
Flamina waits patiently in her tomb.

13.6: In which a dead girl helps herself.

Flamina waits patiently in her tomb.
Meanwhile, Pedro detours to slack his thirst.
Just one glass (then four more) does he consume,
'til so full of wine his belly might burst.

Instead of rescue, seems Pedro has napped.
Flamina wakes up inside her coffin.
It's dark, cold, and cramped, and she's feeling trapped.
Thinks to herself, "Men fail me so often."

Puts her back into it, opens the lid.
Clad in just a nightgown, with her feet bare,
removes the shroud, puts on the clothes she hid,
runs off into the chilly night air.

Meantime, on her way for an aperitif,
Isabelle is in danger from a thief.

13.7: In which a maiden receives an unwanted proposal.

Isabelle is in danger from a thief.
She's Oratio's sister (Dottore's her dad).
That night she sneaks out to get some relief
from her beau, Flavio. Wants him real bad.

But before they meet, she runs into a rogue.
A scoundrel known as 'The Captain' lies in wait.
A lass like Isabelle is quite in vogue,
so at sword point says, "Let's go on a date!"

He's faster than Isabelle, no contest.
She's carried away over his shoulder.
She kicks and she screams and beats on his chest.
But yet, in his firm grasp does he hold her.

There's one more subplot (at least I assume):
Harlequin seeks riches amid the gloom.

13.8: In which a graverobber plies his disreputable trade.

Harlequin seeks riches amid the gloom.
Pantaloon's valet's not above robbing graves.
Isabelle's crypt he is off to exhume.
Maybe it's filled with the treasures he craves?

Once inside, though, there is nothing of worth.
The coffin's been opened; there's just her shroud.
The burial garment is stained with earth
but could bring a few scudi... He's not proud.

He is carrying it back home to his lair
when he crosses Flamina in the street.
Assumes she's a ghost! Gives him quite a scare!
Drops the shroud and flees as his bowels excrete.

Now back to Isabelle and the blackguard.
Escaping a kidnapper can be hard.

13.9: In which Isabelle escapes her captor.

Escaping a kidnapper can be hard,
but Isabelle is made of hardy stock.
She waits until the Captain drops his guard
then clobbers the pest with a nearby rock.

She flees down the street. There's no place to hide.
Comes 'cross the death shroud that Harlequin dropped.
Puts it on, pretends to be one who died.
The Captain arrives. In his tracks he's stopped.

He thinks Isabelle is a poltergeist.
"It's Flamina's spirit haunting the town!"
The Captain's hands grow cold; his feet are iced.
He runs away, several times falling down.

The job done, she drops her Flamina mask.
Escaping a tomb is a grueling task.

13.10: In which a dead girl seeks directions.

Escaping a tomb is a grueling task.
And once you do, you still have to walk home.
Flamina takes a large swig from her flask.
She's lost, grumpy, and continues to roam.

She stumbles upon Isabelle yelling
at some coward who is fleeing, afeared.
She asks, "Could you help me find my dwelling?"
Isabelle thinks Flamina's ghost appeared!

Isabelle runs off without the death shroud.
Flamina follows her, "Wait, wait! Don't go."
Isabelle can't hear her; she's screaming too loud.
Who comes 'cross the garment next? It's Pedro.

He drunkenly dons it with disregard.
Seeing a ghost can leave anyone scarred.

13.11: In which three paranormal encounters are described.

Seeing a ghost can leave anyone scarred,
especially back in the late middle-age.
Three scaredy-cats end up in Pantaloon's yard,
each with a story when they come onstage.

"Captain saw Flamina!" he shouts, trembling.
Harlequin cries, "From her tomb she's released!"
Isabelle chimes in, "Ghosts are assembling...
They're craving our souls. We must find a priest!"

Pantaloon and Dottore don't believe.
But then again... three stories consistent.
And there's no reason for them to deceive.
When they're questioned, the three are insistent.

The 'ghost' stumbles by, lugging a wine cask.
Could there be a *Zanni* under that mask?

13.12: In which the ghostly spirit's true nature is revealed.

Could there be a *Zanni* under that mask?
None present are valiant enough to look.
Won't pull on its shroud; too scared to ask.
Pantaloon and Dottore seemed quite shook.

The Captain ran away into the night.
Isabelle cowers behind her daddy.
Harlequin and the rest tremble with fright.
Only Flavio will face this baddie.

He steps forth, with bravery grabs the cloak.
Unmasks the ghost. It's just Pedro smirking.
In his drunken stupor, thought it a joke.
Flamina's spirit was never out lurking.

From their terror they have now recovered.
Flavio's bravery is then discovered.

13.13: In which a valiant young man is betrothed.

Flavio's bravery is then discovered.
No one can handle a ghost like this lad!
The truth of the prank he has uncovered.
His nerve and his daring are ironclad.

Dottore's impressed. He gives a reward.
"My boy, I know you seek my daughter's hand...
In Isabelle's eyes, you are adored...
I think you should give her a wedding band."

All cheer the betrothal of the cute pair.
It's a great match. They'll get married today.
Seems all's well that ends well in this affair.
But... of the main characters of this play –

Where did Flamina go? Under cover?
Where is the maiden's true faithful lover?

13.14: IN WHICH A DEAD GIRL IS RESURRECTED.

Where is the maiden's true faithful lover?
Remember that guy? Oratio was his name.
Soon he emerges from the ground cover,
holding the hand of his eternal flame.

"Yes," Flamina tells them all, "I'm not dead...
T'was nothing more than an elaborate ruse.
In the meantime, we snuck off and were wed...
Too late to protest, but here, have some booze."

Pantaloon's so grateful his daughter's alive.
He shares in the toast, even pops a cork.
"I'm sorry your love I sought to deprive...
Here's hoping you're soon visited by a stork!"

There's no use in separating a lover.
Innamorati will meet under cover.

13: MASTERSONNET:

Innamorati will meet under cover.
It's not that often one finds a soulmate.
Will her forlorn suitor e'er recover?
Oratio'll help Flamina avoid fate.

Dottore helps comfort Pantaloon's grief.
Flamina waits patiently in her tomb.
Isabelle is in danger from a thief.
Harlequin seeks riches amid the gloom.

Escaping a kidnapper can be hard.
Escaping a tomb is a grueling task.
Seeing a ghost can leave anyone scarred.
Could there be a *Zanni* under that mask?

Flavio's bravery is then discovered.
Where is the maiden's true faithful lover?

HARLEQUIN

Crown No. 14:

"The Faithful Pilgrim Lover"

14.1: In which an untamable woman is introduced.

Where is the maiden's true, faithful lover?
Well, that's a story for another day.
Just kidding. 'Tis what we're sure to cover
by the time we reach the end of this play.

'*The Faithful Pilgrim Lover*' this one's called.
Flavio's the one referenced in the name.
He seeks to wed Isabelle. She's appalled.
"Barefoot and pregnant? No way! That's too tame!"

She craves an adventure on the high seas.
Never content as a stay-at-home wife.
And while many times Flavio says, "Please,"
she won't accept a traditional life.

Though her father seems quite fond of the lad,
she refused to leave it up to her dad.

14.2: In which a maiden seeks freedom on the high seas.

She refused to leave it up to her dad.
Won't stay in Milan under Dottore.
Flavio's handsome, but it makes her sad
that father seeks to write her life story.

So her father's betrothal she declined.
Packed up a few things and ran away.
Left Flavio and Dottore behind;
a Genoese caravel sat in the bay...

They don't allow ladies on board their ship,
so Isabelle must go incognito.
From bodice and corset, she does now strip.
She's soon dressed as a boy named 'Fabrito.'

In Genoa, a new life she'll discover.
With Oratio, she'll go undercover.

256

14.3: In which a servant provides romantic advice.

With Oratio, she'll go undercover.
The Genoese prince needs a manservant.
Hires 'Fabrito,' treats him like a brother.
Sees naught amiss (he's not that observant).

This prince loves Flamina, thinks she smells nice.
Winning her hand is his life's ambition.
He asks his worldly friend for some advice
but 'Fabrito' reacts with derision.

"Love is naught but a sucker's game, my lord...
You are far better off alone and free...
Flamina's charms are best left unexplored."
But the young, lovesick prince does not agree.

So Oratio debates with his comrade;
he loves love, while 'Fabrito' thinks it's bad.

14.4: In which a servant schemes to liberate his master.

He loves love, while 'Fabrito' thinks it's bad.
But how to convince the Prince of its folly?
'Fabrito' decides a ruse must be had
to make Oratio a bit melancholy.

"If he knows she's unfaithful," 'Fabrito' schemes,
"He will realize love's pointless and boring...
Then he will be free to follow our dreams...
To travel the globe, freely exploring."

Can't taste life's pleasures tied down to a spouse!
Want a new romance in every port!
Can't wake up each morning in the same house!
Rather sail the seas, fight lions for sport!

By now I bet you know what comes next, folks...
The disguised servant plans a heartless hoax.

14.5: IN WHICH A LUSTY RUSE IS IMPRUDENTLY UNDERTAKEN.

The disguised servant plans a heartless hoax.
Isabelle's well-aware of how men seduce.
Won't be too hard for 'Fabrito' to coax
Flamina into becoming quite loose.

A jaunty beret, wide-open doublet,
would surely cause Flamina's heart to stir.
Tight trousers will show off his best asset
and, of course, a splash of clove oil and myrrh.

'Fabrito' complements Flamina's eyes.
Gifts her a package of Turkish delights.
Compares the girl's beauty to a sunrise.
Shows off how sculpted his legs look in tights.

A last touch – a love letter is written.
It works too well! Flamina is smitten.

14.6: In which a seduction is more successful than expected.

It works too well, Flamina is smitten.
Fabrito's plump lips, his soft hairless chin
starts Flamina purring like a kitten.
Something about 'him' makes her want to sin.

She visits Oratio's when she knows he's gone.
Fabrito's alone. Now's the time to indulge.
Pins him to the wall, begs for his... falchion.
Her gown slips off and she grabs for his bulge.

Flamina is fumbling with his codpiece
when Oratio returns unexpected.
Finds fiancé and friend in wild caprice
so he flees down the street, quite dejected.

Oratio's heartbroken; he cries and chokes,
not realizing it was only a joke.

14.7: In which an unusual pilgrim arrives in Genoa.

Not realizing it was only a joke,
Oratio ends Act One reeling in shock.
The stage is reset (in a style baroque) –
Act Two begins on the Genoese dock –

Flavio's disembarking a carrack.
He's wearing plain robes; his scalp is close-shorn.
His few possessions are stored in a sack.
Becoming a monk was his way to mourn.

Though he tells people Isabelle's deceased
and he's on a pilgrimage in her name,
he's not seeking the Holy Land in the east;
he's searching the world for that crazy dame.

Everywhere he goes, from Crete to Britain,
Flavio's wearing a mask to fit in.

14.8: In which a pilgrim receives disquieting news.

Flavio's wearing a mask to fit in,
but so is Isabelle for that matter.
In a tavern, Fabrito's just sittin',
vexed that Oratio's heart she did shatter.

Flavio doesn't know Fabrito's a 'she.'
Sits down beside him. Shares his sorry tale.
Then Flavio asks, "Did you ever see…
My love Isabelle, the perfect female?"

Isabelle is offended he won't quit.
Can't Flavio take 'no' for an answer?
She lies to his face; on the floor she does spit.
"Your Isabelle's really dead! T'was cancer!"

Preposterous? Yes, but she's costumed well –
Not obvious Fabrito's Isabelle.

14.9: In which an untamable woman feels regret.

Not obvious Fabrito's Isabelle,
and so he believes him (why would he not?)
Knowing he's come too late makes him unwell.
"Without her love, this life I'll boycott!"

He asks directions to the nearest bridge.
"I'll jump to my death and my beloved join."
He quickly departs – to his life... abridge,
tossing 'Fabrito' a handful of coin.

'Fabrito' feels a strange new emotion.
Flavio was an inspiring guy.
Brave enough to cross over an ocean.
Was it wrong to let him just go and die?!?

As she grapples with passions long suppressed,
Isabelle's dad is still feeling depressed.

14.10: In which distressed father arrives in Genoa.

Isabelle's dad is still feeling depressed
and arrives in town mere minutes later
still searching for his daughter. He won't rest
'til he finds her (and that guy who'd date her).

Comes across a beautiful man sobbing.
"Good Sir, what's wrong?" he says to the fellow.
'Fabrito' looks up. While his eyes need daubing;
he's like a sculpture by Donatello.

"Dad, it's me, Isabelle! Since I left, it's been tough...
I'm *en travesty* (dressed up as a boy)...
Seems Flavio died 'cause of my rebuff...
A noble and true love did I destroy!

Dottore tries to his daughter's tears quell
while on her love-life Flamina does dwell.

14.11: In which Flamina regrets her indiscretion.

While on her love-life Flamina does dwell,
she heads to the bar to get drunk on meade.
Oratio's great! (You could say he was swell.)
Did she mess things up with her lusty deed?

Overhears 'Fabrito,' that lecherous cad.
He's talking to someone about suicide.
Doesn't know it's Isabelle and her dad.
Thinks they said it's Oratio who died!

Upset her betrayal led to this place.
How could she be tempted by 'Fabrito'?
She slaps him hard in his beautiful face.
(He's so fair she can't stay mad at him though.)

Just when the players are at their most stressed,
Flavio returns from his fruitless quest.

14.12: In which Fabrito's true nature is revealed.

Flavio returns from his fruitless quest.
Seems the Ligurian Sea's not that deep.
He's soggy and muddy and half-undressed,
but he's alive! Isabelle starts to weep.

He didn't go through with drowning for love.
Dottore tells him Isabelle's not dead.
"In fact, she's right in front of you, sort of..."
'Fabrito' takes the toupee of his head.

...And there before them, fair Isabelle stands.
"Flavio, my pilgrim, let's get married...
And united, we'll sail to distant lands...
Enjoying experiences varied."

Fabrito's reveal causes some dismay...
Flamina thinks on how she went astray.

14.13: In which the script flirts with being too
        progressive.

Flamina thinks on how she went astray.
And look, in this play, we can't get graphic.
(It's the Renaissance, there's not much leeway,)
But does Flamina have feelings... sapphic?

Just then, Oratio bursts in with his stick.
"I've come to fight for the hand of Flamina!...
Wait? What is this?!? Fabrito... You're a chick?"
And problem's solved by deus ex machina.

"Oratio is alive?!?" Flamina screams,
"While I've had impure thoughts, I must confess...
Marry me, you are the man of my dreams!...
(Although... maybe... could you try on this dress?)"

No moral this play is meant to convey.
No one will learn a lesson here today.

14.14: IN WHICH THE CURTAIN CLOSES AT THE FINALE.

No one will learn a lesson here today.
Together, four lovers will tour the world.
They head to the docks, and anchors away!
The curtain comes down like a sail unfurled.

The players all return to take a bow.
Vecchi, *Zanni*, and *Innamorati*, alike.
With a quaint curtsy, blown kiss, and a 'ciao',
they tell you to leave and go take a hike.

In Commedia, things always end fine.
The girl always gets to marry her crush.
The oppressed underclass always will shine.
Pompous, blowhard misers always get hushed.

I hope you agree that we did cover
where was the maiden's true faithful lover.

14: MASTERSONNET:

Where is the maiden's true, faithful lover?
She refused to leave it up to her dad.
With Oratio, she'll go undercover.
He loves love, but Fabrito thinks it's bad.

The disguised servant plans a heartless hoax.
It works too well; Flamina's smitten.
Not realizing it was only a joke,
Flavio puts on a mask to fit in.

Not obvious Fabrito is Isabelle,
Isabelle's dad is still feeling depressed.
While on her love-life Flamina does dwell.
Flavio returns from his fruitless quest.

Flamina thinks on how she went astray.
No one will learn a lesson here today.

Grandmastersonnet

No one will learn a lesson here today.
On stage are two lovers, and a cuckold.
It's only Commedia dell'arte!
Improvising off a script that's quite old.

They are just performers in a light play,
uttering their ad-libbed lines, tongue in cheek.
Some jokes are tame, some bawdy and risqué.
"Please let us practice our improv technique!"

A *Vecchio* is an old rich buffoon.
Devious servants comprise the *Zanni*.
In this tale, the Captain and Pantaloon
watch Pedro perform some trick uncanny.

Innamorati will meet under cover.
Where is the maiden's true, faithful lover?

Glossary

APENNINE MOUNTAINS: The mountain range that runs through the Italian peninsula.

ARLECCHINA: A Commedia character, and member of the Zanni. A gender-swapped version of Arlecchino (Harlequin). *See,* Harlequin.

ARLECCHINO: *See,* Harlequin.

DR. BALOARDO: A Commedia character, and variant of il Dottore. His name roughly translates to 'Doctor Idiot.'

BATTACIO: A stick, baton, or club that Commedia characters often used to beat and slap each other with. The origin of the modern word 'slapstick.'

BRIGHELLA: A Commedia character, and member of the Zanni. He is less stupid and more violent than most other Zanni. His name roughly translates to "someone who bothers others."

BOSPORUS STRAIT: The body of water connecting the Black Sea and the Mediterranean. Location of modern-day Istanbul (Constantinople).

BUSS: An archaic word that means kiss.

CADUCEUS: The traditional symbol of a medical doctor. A staff with two snakes on it.

CARAVEL: A small, fast Spanish or Portuguese sailing ship of the 15th–17th centuries.

CARRACK: A large sailing ship used to transport cargo long distances in the 14th–15th centuries.

THE CAPTAIN (IL CAPITANO SPAVENTA): A Commedia character, and member of the Vecchi. Often an antagonist, the Captain is boastful, pompous, and violent, but also cowardly when challenged. He is usually extremely opportunistic and greedy. However, he is sometimes a brave Innamorato. He usually wore an over-the-top military uniform and waved a sword. He had multiple personal names over the years, the most popular being Spaventa, which translates to 'Captain Fearsome' (and is meant to be taken ironically).

CATHAY: An archaic term for China.

COQUETTE: An archaic term for a flirtatious woman.

COLUMBINE (COLUMBINA): A Commedia character, and member of the Zanni. Usually a servant or a peasant. Her character is rather bold and uncouth compared to other female characters. She can also be rather lusty at times. Unlike most Zanni, she is competent, often the only functional intellect on the stage. Her name translates to 'little dove.' The character is also known by the name Franceschina, which the name Scala used in his work.

CONDOTTIERE: An Italian mercenary during the Italian Wars fought during the Renaissance. Literally translates to 'someone under contract.'

CONTESSA: The Italian word for countess.

COVIELLO: A Commedia character, and member of the Zanni.

DESTRIER: A type of large horse used in calvary warfare.

DOGE: The title ascribed to the ruler of Venice during the time it was an independent city state.

DONATELLO: Donato di Niccolò di Betto Bardi was a Florentine sculptor (1386–1466).

IL DOTTORE GRATIANO: A Commedia character and member of the Vecchi. The title of Dottore means doctor, but in the general sense (not specifically a medical doctor). He is rich and highly educated, although not very smart. He is often the foil to Pantaloné, and the parent to one of the Innamorati. His costume is usually all or mostly black and he frequently wears a black felt hat with long, trailing robes, like a judge. He had multiple names over the years, the most popular being Gratiano, and he appears in Shakespeare's play '*The Merchant of Venice.*'

DUCATI: The currency used in the Venetian Republic during the Renaissance.

EN TRAVESTY: A Commedia term that means to dress in the clothes of the opposite sex (usually as a disguise).

FABRITO: Not quite an independent Commedia character, but the alias usually used by a female character who has disguised herself as a man (en travesty).

FALCHION: A type of large sword popular in Europe during the Middle Ages.

FLAMINA: A Commedia character and member of the Innamorati. Usually the daughter of a Vecchio. Flamina never wore a mask and was dressed in the highest fashions of the day.

FLAVIO: A Commedia character, and member of the Innamorati. Usually the son of a Vecchio. Flavio never wore a mask and was dressed in the highest fashions of the day.

FLORINS: The currency used in Florence during the Renaissance.

GIANDUJA: A Commedia character, and member of the Zanni.

GRANDEE: A Spanish or Portuguese nobleman of high rank.

GRATIANO: *See,* Dottore.

HARLEQUIN: A Commedia character, and member of the Zanni. Harlequin is characterized by his checkered costume. His role is that of a light-hearted, nimble, and astute servant, often acting to thwart the plans of his master, and pursuing his own love interest, Columbine. The character is also known by the name Arlecchino, which is the name Scala used in his work.

HOI POLLOI: An archaic term for the common people.

INNAMORATI: A Commedia term for two star-crossed lovers. They went by many names over the years, but usually did not have distinct personality traits, unlike Vecchi and Zanni. In this work, Flamina, Isabelle, Oratio, and Flavio are the main Innamorati. Most Commedia plots revolve around attempts to get the Innamorati together. They are ridiculous and over the top about everything, but they are completely sincere in their emotions. Unlike most Commedia characters, Innamorati never wore masks or had specific costumes, they were just dressed in the highest fashions of the day.

INTERMEZZO: Italian for 'intermission.'

ISABELLE (ISABELLA): A Commedia character, and member of the Innamorati. Usually the daughter of a Vecchio. She was sometimes portrayed as tender and loving but other times more flirtatious and strong-willed compared to an average Innamorati. Isabella never wore a mask and was dressed in the highest fashions of the day.

ITALIAN WARS: A series of conflicts between medieval city-states that took place in Italy and other parts of Europe from 1494 to 1559.

LA SIGNORA: A Commedia character, and member of the Vecchi. Usually a bored housewife of a rich merchant. La Signora is a title, not her given name.

LAZZO (PL. LAZZI): A Commedia term for a short bit of entertainment inserted into a performance, yet not directly tied to the plot. It can be a specific joke or catchphrase associated with a specific character, or a bit of physical humor like slipping on a banana. It can also be a talent, like juggling, playing a lute, or performing acrobatics.

LIGURIAN SEA: The body of water off the coast of Genoa.

LINDOR: A Commedia character, and member of the Innamorati.

MEADE: An alcoholic beverage made by fermenting honey.

MEZZETINO: A Commedia character, and member of the Zanni. A variant of Brighella. His name means 'Half-Measure (of liquor).'

MODIGLIANI: Amedeo Modigliani was an Italian painter and sculptor (1884–1920).

La Ruffiana: A Commedia character, and member of the Vecchi. La Ruffiana is a title, not her given name. Usually portrayed as a gossip.

Rosine: A Commedia character, and member of the Innamorati.

Oratio: A Commedia character, and member of the Innamorati. Usually the son of a Vecchio. Oratio never wore a mask and was dressed in the highest fashions of the day.

Pantaloon (Pantalone): A Commedia character, and member of the Vecchi. His is usually portrayed as old, rich, miserly, and oblivious. He often has an inappropriate enthusiasm for young ladies who do not reciprocate his interest. He is often a parent to one of the Innamorati, and the master to a Zanni. He is also usually a foil to il Dottore. His costume is made of elaborate, expensive-looking clothes all colored red. 'Pantaloons,' an archaic term for pants, comes from this character.

Pasquale (Pasquella): A Commedia character, and member of the Zanni. Sometimes a servant, sometimes a wife, and sometimes even a witch or fortuneteller.

Pedro (Pedrolino): A Commedia character, and member of the Zanni. Often a peasant or servant to a Vecchio. Pedrolino is usually the social wit and willing servant who survives by serving others, although usually with an eye towards how he could spin events for personal gain. He can be a protagonist who helps the Innamorati, or just a selfish agent of chaos. His name means 'Little Peter.' Pedrolino is most often dressed in an all-white wardrobe with exaggeratedly over-sized and loose-fitting clothes, typically including a white jacket with large buttons and comically long sleeves, a large neck ruff, and a large, floppy hat. He is considered to be an early inspiration for the modern day white-faced clown.

PRIVY: An archaic term for a bathroom.

PULCINELLA: A Commedia character, and member of the Zanni. Often a perverted bumpkin who also walks with a limp. His name roughly translates to 'young chicken' because of his odd, bird-like way of walking.

SCALA: Flaminio Scala was a famous Commedia actor, known for playing the role of Flavio. He was also the author of *Il teatro delle favole rappresentative*, a handbook of famous Commedia scenarios published in 1611, which formed the basis for these sonnets.

SANDRONÉ: A Commedia character, and member of the Zanni. He is usually portrayed as the spokesman of the underclass.

SCAPINO: A Commedia character, and member of the Zanni. A variant of Brighella. His name roughly translates to 'someone who escapes.'

SCARAMOUCHE: A Commedia character, and member of the Zanni. Often boastful and cowardly, he was an underclass version of il Capitano.

SCUDI (S. SCUDO): A currency used in various Italian city-states during the Renaissance.

SCULLERY: An archaic term for a laundry or dishwashing room.

SESTIERE: One of any six administrative divisions of Venice.

SPADA: A type of sword popular in Italy during the Renaissance.

SPAVENTA: *See,* Il Capitano.

SPONTOON: A type of weapon similar to a spear or a halberd.

TARTAGLIA: A Commedia character. Sometimes an Innamorato, a Vecchio, or even a Zanni. He is known for having bad vision and a stutter.

TINO (BURRATINO): A Commedia character, and member of the Zanni. Usually a good-natured house servant, an innkeeper, a gardener, a peasant, a beggar, or a long-lost father. He is also often gluttonous. He usually wears a flat, round hat. His name translates to 'little donkey.'

TREVI FOUNTAIN: A famous fountain in Rome. While the elaborate fountain that exists today was built in the 1800s, a fountain existed at that location in some form as far back as 19 B.C.E.

TURKISH DELIGHTS: A sugary candy made with jelly, nuts, and fruits.

IL VECCHI (s. VECCHIO): A Commedia term for the class of characters that are old, rich, and pompous. They are usually the antagonists of the story but can sometimes be wise and helpful benefactors. The word means 'old one' in Italian. The primary members of this group are Pantalone, il Dottore, and il Capitano.

VIELLE: An archaic instrument similar to a violin or a viola.

ZANNI: A Commedia term for the class of characters that are members of the underclass or servants. They can sometimes be the protagonist or a competent assistant, but they can also be lazy drunkards or mischievous criminals. The primary members of this group are Pedrolino, Arlecchino (Harlequin), and Pulcinella.

A Series of Small Heartbreaks

If you actually find yourself enjoying the concept of absurd tales written in formalist sonnet form, you might want to seek out the author's other, book: <u>A Series of Small Heartbreaks</u>.

Classic formalism meets modern themes in this collection of 160 mischievous sonnets. Every sonnet in this collection is structured in the oldest and stodgiest "Petrarchan" form, but each one tells a disarmingly dumb (yet emotionally devastating) tale of teen romance, time-machines, regret, doomsday devices, love, loss, longing, the horrors of war, murderous Santas, lonely sea captains, mortality, errant rocketships, existentialism, melancholy ghosts, dumb humor, monstrous tardigrades, devastating breakups, zombies, the lump in your throat as you watch the perfect opportunity to express your love pass by, and the eventual heat death of the universe.

Available on Amazon and other major bookstores.

ISBN: 978-1-931468-37-4

www.ingramcontent.com/pod-product-compliance
Lightning Source LLC
Chambersburg PA
CBHW040421110426

42813CB00014B/2723